CRADLE OF BITCHIN

*A Story of Mentors, Watermen,
& the Sea*

Hope you enjoy it !

Lee
(Twiigs) '58

William Sentar

In the sea alone,
frozen to the bone,
waiting, waiting,
for the one to carry me home.

The cold wind on my back, cruel,
The water an unsavory gruel,
waiting, waiting
for the one to carry me home.

I cannot explain the feeling I had,
but somehow I could feel her coming,
The one to carry me home.

And then I saw her,
First rising, ever so gently,
ever so increasing in might,
I paddled like hell,
to catch the swell,
She was the one to carry me home.

Standing now in the icy wind,
I somehow no longer feel cold.
To my right a gleaming green wall,
While a roaring caldron chases my heels.

The green wall is gone now,
in her place the smooth white foam.
inside I smile a "thank you"
for the one that carried me home

When I think of what I gave for
that one wave,
a tear wells in my eye,
For although she's long gone to
her grave,
in my heart she will never die.

June 6, 1960 Surfing Magazine

CRADLE OF BITCHIN

*A Story of Mentors, Watermen,
& the Sea*

by

A. LEE BROWN

AUTHOR'S NOTE ~ The following pages attempt to place hours of historical research, personal discussions, and experiences into a textual blender that produces a story of general interest worth telling. Aware of the tendency of old men to indulge in feebleminded ramblings of "back-in-the-day," an oath was taken to avoid personal pronouns like "I" or "me" as much as possible. Why? The reason was simple; the purpose of *Cradle* is to share a unique story---not an autobiography. Despite setting that goal, I have failed. Once the writing began, it was clear the voice coming from behind the curtains was mine alone and it was better to allow autobiographical passages to flow rather than be arbitrarily eliminated.

It was also decided to use the true names of individuals and friends (often having nothing in common) whenever possible.

Library of Congress Cataloging-in-Publication Data
Brown, A. Lee; ISBN-13: 979-8-218-11523-4 (paperback)

Published by Eight Bells Press

REFLECTIONS

Bill Chapman–cradle surfer, author, musician (PLHS '63)
From getting pummeled in Ocean Beach's shore break at age three to still surfing there 75 years later, I never get over the uniqueness of the place and the luck us kids had to begin life there. Brown captures some of the best stories and characters of those times, not only with the make-it-all-fun attitude of the surf kids and capturing the eccentricities of the setting, but also placing it within the context of what was happening in global history at the time. A fun and educating read from start to end.

Steve Aldridge-cradle surfer, merchant, musician (PLHS '56)
Having grown up in The Cradle, I can say those were the most wonderful carefree days of my life; the beach and ocean were my whole world. There's something about the ocean that always draws me back...I can't explain it other than it is mystical. Lee's book is an intriguing story that I call---Pretty Bitchin.

Richard Arnold-cradle surfer/beach boy, pilot, sculptor (PLHS '59)
My dad died when I was five and the Ocean Beach lifeguards became my surrogate fathers. Those fellows taught me how to harvest and respect the sea and the way of the Waterman. As I look back to those times I realize I could never have had a more bitchin childhood.

Robert Wineteer-Windansea surfer, entrepreneur (LJHS '59)
Lee Brown accurately describes a unique era that a few of us were lucky enough to experience. It is a story involving our mentors and their spirit of Aloha which had a great influence on us by setting the waterman's way of life never to be equaled again. By reading this book you will get an idea of what a fabulous time this was.

Sam Cody-cradle surfer, graphic artist. (PLHS '63)
Wow! What a journey! To be a part of this group of friends...I'm very stoked! Very humbled! Being at the right place and time created a good life with the friends I met during that era. Thank you Lee.

Dave DeVore-cradle surfer, Superior Court Judge (PLHS '62)
A fondness for one's formative years may not be unique, but for those of us who came of age in Ocean Beach there was a special quality to it. Lee and I shared the ocean during a time when age differences weren't important and the Pacific was our incubator that created a bond still in existence seven decades later. It is what Lee rightfully characterizes as "The Cradle" of our youth.

Doug Smith-lifeguard, mentor, beach boy, realtor (PLHS '53)
Growing up in Ocean Beach was more like a family. It was a life of clean living and always adventurous by surfing, swimming, diving and occasional fish and ab fries which culminated in every aspect into a bitchin lifestyle. Lee's book captures the essence of the Cradle.

Alex Caldwell-cradle surfer, physician (PLHS '66)
My dad and his friends were well-known watermen around Point Loma for many years. Following in his tradition, I joined the Sunset Cliffs Surf Club in 1966. The names that Lee mentions in CRADLE were fellows I knew and surfed with as well. One of my best memories was swinging a pickaxe to build the steps at the foot of Ladera St. for access to the reef breaks below. At first, the City tried to destroy our work but it eventually recognized surfing as an asset. But let me be clear, beach life before the Hollywood movies was still the best!

DEDICATIONS

Kathryn Brown
Life's Co-Author

Tracey Brown
Editor & Bitchin Daughter

Shelby Brown
Family "Consigliere" & Bitchin Son

Mentors

Steve Aldridge, Bob Baxley*, Bob Cosgrove*, Mike Considine*, Ed Hoffman, Hal Krupens*, Rod Luscomb*, Sonny Maggoria, Terry and Bill Martin, Marsh* and Ray Malcolm*, Don Mellon*, Lance Morton*, Bill Norton*, Alan Pollock, Jim Richards, Jim Robb*, Tony Roenicke, Doug Smith*, Gordon Tribby, Winnie Ward, Greg Widders*

(* = ocean lifeguards)

OTHER BOOKS

Rules & Conflict (Prentice Hall)

Brief History of Political Theory
(Grossmont College Press)

The Varsity (Eight Bells Press)

CONTENTS

PROLOGUE 1

PREMISE 3

PART I ~ *FOUNDATIONS* 7

Generations 9

Language 13

Location 19

Liquid 25

Cradle's Campuses 29

PART II ~ *BEACH LIFE* 47

New Horizons 49

Contests 61

Shorts 73

Cribs 83

Lifeguards 87

Kamu A'O ~ Mentors 93

Hodads, Jacket Clubs, & Night Life 103

Capers & Pranks 109

Sea's Bounty 115

High Country 121

PART III ~ *DIASPORA* 129

Beginning of the End 131

ABOUT THE AUTHOR 137

CREDITS 139

FOREWORD BY DON MELLON

The Cradle of Bitchin tells of a time and place making the reader want to return to that wondrous reality. Lee Brown asserts that being an adolescent, living in a small beach town in southern California during the 1950s and early 60s took on historical proportions. To capture these moments, he draws upon personal experience, academic life, and creative writing skills. By careful use of anecdotal incidents, oceanic adventures, interaction with older mentors, friends, and lifeguarding, he provides a humorous and enlightening portrait of the beach culture of those times.

The author creates a framework that stresses the importance of mentoring in the development of a just and moral culture. He praises the Polynesian tradition of respecting experienced elders for their water skill and willingness to guide and direct a younger generation. Skillfully, Brown rolls the whole ball of wax into a truly enjoyable glimpse of what it was like growing up in the cradle of bitchin-ness.

I, too, was a youngster during these times, and in this locale, who had the good fortune to share a passion for the ocean with friends my age. I grew up in the very beach town described by Lee. My local lifeguard/mentors were an enormous influence upon the values we developed. Like the Polynesian watermen of yore, our mentors taught us ways to be at one with the sea, and this wisdom became a compass for life. Those fellows were larger than life characters who, by their common spirit, taught us to chase the elusive enchantment of the sea.

The spirit of the *Cradle* is captured in the watercolor painting on page 46 where the bamboo shack and lifeguard tower capture the heart of the cradle. Lee and I lifeguarded the beaches of San Diego, which makes him exceptionally qualified to tell this story. For the reader, *The Cradle of Bitchin* is a clean, fresh breeze from the coast.

Don Mellon was born in Ocean Beach, attended its schools and graduated (1952) from Point Loma High. Mellon was an ocean lifeguard and later enlisted in the U.S. Army, and trained as a paratrooper who saw combat in Korea with 187th Airborne. At war's end, Don returned to the lifeguard service while attending San Diego State. Later, he pursued successful careers in finance and commercial real estate development and, more recently, began writing both fiction and non-fiction available with booksellers across America. My favorite is Migrant Dog (2020).

PROLOGUE

O ver a long academic career, I authored scientific treatises, textbooks, articles, and novels, yet what follows is the story of which I am most proud. Why? Because *Cradle of Bitchin* has a three-fold purpose: first, to provide a glimpse into a unique and little known period of American cultural history that spread to influence the rest of the nation; second, to acknowledge the positive role mentors can contribute for adolescents; and, lastly, to bring a little humor and joy to a world pulverized relentlessly by troubling events. In a word, the *Cradle of Bitchin* contends how willing elders can contribute to help adolescents navigate the dangerous shoals on their voyage to maturity. As a result, these individuals led us to experience one of the most wonderful times in human history.

Centuries ago, a teacher named Plato was often surrounded by Athenian youth beseeching him to explain the nature of the Good, the True, and the Beautiful. Had he re-appeared in Ocean Beach, California in, say, 1955, I suspect the Greek philosopher would have been pleasantly surprised! Why? Because after all those centuries, it was still possible to find a small group of men interacting with youthful listeners discussing the connection between living in ethical harmony with their environment and each other.

Lastly, a word about Wahines. Missing from this story is a separate discussion of how girls and young women figured into the beach culture of the times. To be honest, during the 1950s and early 1960s, very few females in Ocean Beach ventured beyond the shoreline. This isn't to say there were no "Waterwomen" in Ocean Beach six decades ago. For example, Norma Jean Malcolm was an athletic woman, surfer and champion water skier. As time went by, a few more came forward as Judy Dibble or Sara Nelson although they did so more in the 1960s. Linda Benson lived briefly in Point Loma and, at age 15, won the 1959 women's championship at the Makaha International, then returned north to Encinitas. Joyce Hoffman was a fiercely competitive blonde who lived in Capistrano Beach and garnered multiple trophies in the mid to late 1960s; she also became California's first female ocean lifeguard. In the following decades, women from other places appeared like Margo Oberg, Lynne Boyer, and Wendy Botha in the 1970s, 80s, and 90s. Trying to locate and interview women who did adopt the sea

1

A. Lee Brown

as a way of life in Ocean Beach during the 1950s, however, wasn't so easy.

PREMISE

NO MATTER WHAT THE SOURCE, today's news isn't so good is it? Whether we learn about events from the internet, newspapers, texts, cable television or over the back fence, the world seems to be a mess; an infinite ribbon of awfulness ranging from merely disturbing to downright frightening.

Perhaps this state of affairs shouldn't come as a surprise, especially since western civilization's roots are sunk deeply in the inherent pessimism of the Judeo-Christian tradition. Consider, for example, St. Augustine's declaration 1,600 years ago that, "*...the whole human race has been condemned in its first origin, this life itself, if life it is to be called, bears witness by the host of cruel ills with which it is filled.*" Even America's own Founding Fathers were petrified by the darker side of humanity as stated by James Madison when he said the causes of human discord "*...are sown in the nature of man.*"

Who knows if our woes are caused by human nature, the devil, or death rays from Ming the Merciless? The fact remains, we are pounded relentlessly by awful conditions that appear to be worsening. No small amount of this misery is tied to a planet with 8 billion inhabitants, most of whom (60 percent) are crammed into large cities. Sometimes mayhem is small peanuts like the fruitcake in Kongsberg, Norway who recently killed his neighbors with a bow and arrows. More often it's larger like the unfathomable madness of Russia's determination to destroy Ukraine's civil society while threatening nuclear war upon anyone who tries to stop them.

Even more disconcerting than the frequency and magnitude of such senselessness, is our growing indifference to the daily trudge of violence and misery. Recent studies of the life cycle of news have found that no matter how horrific an act may be, public interest is brief and tends to wane overnight. Apparently, we're becoming inured to such "breaking news" as North Korea's determination to build and test whopper bombs or shoot missiles over Japan and South Korea; terrorists kidnapping African children; serial forest fires in Siberia and France; suicide bombers in the Middle East; Mexican cartel atrocities in Guanajuato. None of this bad news however, parallels the World

Health Organization's recent estimate that 15 million people perished during the Covid pandemic.

On a global scale, the UN reports its environmental agreement, the Paris Accord, is sputtering. Signed by 196 member nations in 2015, the treaty's goal was to limit the world's average temperature from rising another 1.5 degrees Celsius. Seven years later, however, world temps have risen higher now teetering on the ledge of irreversibility. As a result, record heat swings, unimaginable hurricanes, melting glaciers, floods, and wildfires worsen.

Closer to home, the National Climate Assessment's 2023 draft report---written by hundreds of scientists---recently declared, "...the effects of climate change are worsening throughout the USA...with more extreme events making it harder to maintain safe homes, healthy families, reliable public services, a sustainable economy, and strong communities."

Americans now live in the most materially abundant culture in the history of the world; we possess more gizmos and gadgets than anyone. We are awash in garbage disposals, electric garage door openers, cell phones, and single use plastic. And yet, even in the midst of this copious existence, little evidence exists we are happy or sated. National surveys tell us Americans are more concerned about inflation than record levels of poverty, and boundless immigration. Homeless mortality increased 7 percent over 2021. Young children are being affected increasingly as recent studies have found 72 percent of youngsters 5 to 12 years of age appear overwhelmed by modern conditions, are depressed, and two out of every ten have experienced suicidal thoughts. Even more disturbing, drug usage among school children has become so prevalent schools are now installing naloxone inhalers Estimates of drug related deaths vary, yet the National Institutes of Health recorded 92,000 fatalities in 2020 and another 95,000 associated with booze. In similar fashion, suicides rose to over 45,000 of which 30 percent were gun related.

Speaking of guns, the number of firearms in the USA now exceeds its citizenry; that's 400 million guns, a lethal weapon for every man, woman, transgender, adolescent and newborn. Polls conducted by the National Conference of State Legislatures found 28 states permit public school teachers to carry firearms into the classroom. In 2021, 80 percent of the 24,000 homicides involved firearms and the purchase of semi-automatic handguns outpaces the sales of rifles and shotguns combined. A new concern for law enforcement is the surge in untraceable ghost guns of which 19,000 were confiscated in 2021. This trend shouldn't be too surprising since the annual domestic production of handguns has tripled since 2002, adding 11 million new weapons annually. Amidst such alarming statistics, can mass shootings like those at the Las Vegas Harvest Music Festival, Chicago's Independence Day Parade, Walmart, TOPS Friendly Stores, Sandy Hook and Robb Elementary Schools really surprise anyone?

A century ago, the French sociologist, Émile Durkheim, pioneered the scientific study of social disintegration. When a culture's accepted rules of civility erode, a condition he called *anomie* emerges that replaces human tolerance and respect with indifference, greed, and the clamor for instant gratification.

Is America on the brink of *anomie?* I dunno? But many are beginning to think so, especially when events like the 6JAN violent assault on Congress occurred in the midst of a widespread rise of spite and malice for such traditional institutions as public libraries, school boards, and even the FBI. For the first time in its history, the respected Swedish organization---International Institute for the Study of Democracy--- listed the USA as a country backsliding into authoritarianism in its annual report.

So, one might reasonably ask, how does this state of affairs relate to this book? Puzzled as to why modern discord is so widespread, my thoughts turned inward, "…has it always been like this?" At a personal level my answer is an emphatic NO! Even if my answer is only partially true, it calls for a justification of what made my youth so unique and enjoyable. Such an inquiry means looking beyond the socio-economic conditions of those times as well as the traditional agencies of adolescent training by parents, teachers, peers, religion or media. If we conduct this inquiry in a tight, two-fisted way, it just might be possible to uncover a very positive influence that once guided adolescence.

The premise of *Cradle* rests upon a single proposition: growing up in Ocean Beach, California during the 1950s and early 1960s, was arguably the most wonderful time in history to be young and alive. Although the actress Marion Ross graduated from my high school, the following pages are neither a re-run of her "Happy Days" nor a panacea on how to make the world nicer. Offered instead is a portrait of the social mores, institutions, modes of civility, and the guidance of a group of men who offered a unique and wonderful path to maturity.

A. Lee Brown

In an attempt to examine this contention, the *Cradle of Bitchin* is developed in three, separate, yet linked parts: Foundations; Beach Life; and Diaspora.

A word of caution about what follows. As mentioned previously, *Cradle's* story is not intended to be a memoir. Memoirs clearly have a place in literary circles, but this book's purpose is not to follow the sequential growth of the author over time. True, it offers a lot of personal history which, at times, does not segue easily thus giving the story an appearance of leapfrogging forward and then backward in history. Sometimes this has been unavoidable and every effort has been made to make the flow of time understandable.

When all is said and done, the *Cradle* is a reconstruction of how a number of factors created one of the most wonderful episodes in human history. No small part of this era was what we learned from a slightly older group of beach boys and lifeguards who exposed us to the ways of a Waterman.

PART I ~ *FOUNDATIONS*

Nānā I Ke Kumu

Look to your sense of place and sources
of spirit, and you will find truth

A. Lee Brown

GENERATIONS

DESPITE ATTENDING ALL THE SAME SCHOOLS, we didn't start dating until she was seventeen. At least, by then, I had learned every caring parent likes to autopsy their daughter's suitors very carefully; almost surgically. And so it was, on a warm summer evening in 1962, I stood at my future wife's front door, dreading the *auto-da-fé* to follow.

It didn't take long. Kathy's mother pegged me right away and, without speaking, her countenance announced: flunky beach boy, older, and from the "other" side of Point Loma known as Ocean Beach.

Although it took a bit longer, her father followed suit. Tan and good looking in a Swedish kind of way, he was physically fit, a strong swimmer, avid fisherman, and a man who played tennis regularly on the private courts of friends from other established San Diego families. Adding more degrees of separation to our rapidly un-burgeoning relationship, he'd gone to Berkeley so when the question of my education came up, I knew I was a goner.

Having barely stumbled out of Point Loma High, my attempts at "higher education" had been limited to three, half-hearted, enrollments in the local evening adult school. Ironically, the course that placed me on probation was a "D" in Political Science 10, "American Government for Terminal Students."

In a word, my status was that of an unwanted place holder, a twenty-year-old ocean lifeguard whose only virtues were the ability to endure cold, rough, winter seas and stand erect on a balsa surfboard for limited periods of time. It was as if I'd been sent from central casting at Paramount Studios to audition for Bazarov in Turgenev's novel, *Fathers and Sons;* an interloper destined to upset the household.

Aside from the clear differences in our social circles (plus her dad's disdain of my ignorance of all things worldly and mechanical), this adversity was little more than a variant of an old "saw" about generations. Without hesitation, he accepted the most common of parental delusions: a belief that the morals of one's own generation are superior to all subsequent ones. And so it was, any suggestion I dared

9

to make that perhaps the ethics of my generation were not so much wrong-headed as they were different---was summarily rejected.

Of course, intergenerational condescension has been around for a long time as attested to by screen writers, authors, and historians. Yet this mutual distrust cuts both ways. The young are prone to think of elders as lame and out of touch while, equally culpable, elders are convinced their progeny are lazy, or stupid, or naïve in the ways of the world. Although the notion of "generations" does play a part in what follows, the focus of *Cradle* isn't about

Summary of Recent Generations
Lost Generation ~ Came of age During WWI
Greatest Generation ~ 1900/1927
Silent Generation ~ 1928/1945: "Luckys"
Boomers ~ 1946/1964 "Me" Gen
Gen X ~ 1965/1980: Baby busters
Gen Y ~ 1981/1996: entitled Millennials
Gen Z ~ 1997/2012: Zoomers
Gen Alpha ~ 2013/2025

the acrimony often found between generations. Instead, it is about the unique education passed along by the Pacific Ocean and my elders who took mentoring seriously.

Only recently has my generation been designated as "Lucky" by sociologists. Without a doubt, the uniqueness of those times was partly due to our insularity and protection from social ills commonplace today. My youth (1950s) was defined during an era of unique and quirky humor, unconventional and uncommercialized lifestyle, and bookended by an interlude of world peace and economic stability. Most important, it was an existence in close proximity to the ocean and being introduced to life's challenges by a handful of its habitués; men who oversaw our adjunct education while adopting a supplemental syllabus beyond the structured classroom. Lucky enough to be offered this option, I was soon immersed in the sea's matchless wisdom; a powerful force with its own code of ethics. Learning to respect the sea, its gifts, and unwritten rules of behavior provided a moral compass to safe harbors from the future storms of adversity and absurdity.

Speaking of generational differences, I'd like to pass along a recent incident illustrating the kind of beach etiquette we learned in contrast to more recent times. It involved a misunderstanding between my friend, Jack Thomerson, and another fellow at Terramar Beach just south of Carlsbad, California.

As an aside, Jack had learned to surf in Hawaii as a youngster when his Navy dad was stationed there. A decade later, Jack also became a leatherneck playing service football for the Marine Corps Recruit Depot and later a middle linebacker for San Diego State's Aztecs coached by Don Coryell. In a word, Thomerson is reserved, polite, but, no pansy.

Still surfing in his fifties, Jack was one of the regulars at Terramar break where locals know each other and practice the surfer's common courtesy of alternating rides. One morning, a good surfing, young stranger appeared and proceeded to ignore the local code by taking off in front of other riders any time he could. Having been cut off twice by the interloper, Jack paddled over next to him, sat upright on his board and began to explain why he had allowed this fellow the right of way not once but twice when it wasn't his turn. Not having a lot of sense, the younger man responded, "Listen, Dude, this isn't the 1950s!"

Without a word, the "dude" grabbed the younger man by the collar of his wetsuit, yanked him across his own board and proceeded to spank his "rudeness" to the delight of everyone. Embarrassed and crestfallen, the younger fellow paddled to shore to the applause of the others and was never seen again.

A. Lee Brown

LANGUAGE

A NTHROPOLOGISTS LIKE to discuss drawls, dialects, brogues and slangs. As linguists, they understand how language can shed light on someone's geographic origin, level of education, social status, and race or ethnicity.

To begin, it is helpful to understand there was a difference between the spoken vocabulary of beach goers in the fifties and what was popularized by Hollywood script writers. In the early summer of 1959, Columbia Pictures promised to tell, "The Story of the Beach Generation." Tinsel Town's *Gidget* hit the silver screen starring the pert blond Sandra Dee opposite the male lead of James Darren. It was a film adapted from screen writer Fred Kohner's book about his daughter as she sought to become a surfer on the beaches of Los Angeles. Also cast in the film was the seasoned actor Cliff Robertson as "Big Kahoona." Interestingly, Robertson was born in La Jolla and was the only actor in the film who had surfed in his younger days. The movie was a boffo success raking in $1.5 million. It also incentivized the backlots of Culver City to rollout similar trope films as: *Gidget Goes Hawaiian* (1961); *Blue Hawaii* (1962); *Beach Party* (1963); *Bikini Beach* and *Ride the Wild Surf* (1964); and *Beach Blanket Bingo* (1965).

While a few genuine surfers appeared as stunt doubles, most of the performers were emerging young actors like Frankie Avalon, Elvis Presley, and Walt Disney's famous Mouseketeer, Annette Funicello. Out takes were filmed on Malibu Lagoon and the sands of Balboa, Laguna Beach, and Kauai. Creating a new cinematographic genre, these portrayals were fabricated in the studios of Columbia, Paramount, and American International utilizing an invented vocabulary laced with terms as Cowabunga, Gnarly, Moon Doggy and Boss.

Despite huge box office sales, these films missed the mark with actual surfers. Why? By portraying the surfing life as one, continual, light-hearted romp of bongo parties, a key element was omitted. At the core of stand-up board riding in the 1950s was a deep rejection of existing icons. This "contrarianism" emerged slowly at first, then manifested in more potent ways over time. Take mode of dress, for

13

example. Surfers loved to ransack Goodwill and Salvation Army for anything discarded and outrageous to assemble their sartorial wardrobe. Trim and fit bathing suits, so popular in the swimming pools of the Midwest, were rejected for the haute couture of baggy oversized swim trunks.

Likewise, surfers at Windansea, Pacific Beach, and Ocean Beach turned to sources of entertainment far from the mainstream of accepted American humor. Of course, behind all this ingenuity, was the youthful urge to define itself as different. Bearing this in mind, unpacking a little beach lingo of the 1950s will help: *bad, bitchin,* and *waterman.*

BAD ~ Nowhere, was the beach's alternative lifestyle more evident than in its vocabulary. For example, take the word "bad." Generally speaking, "bad" is an adjective conveying a negative connation. As used in the inverted argot of the fifties surfing culture, however, "bad" meant good! In fact, the badder it was, the gooder it was! If John Casey happened to drive by in his lowered 1954 Ford Club Coupe, someone might mutter, "John's got a bad short;" translation---John has a nice car.

BITCHIN ~ From all the words of my youth, one that maintains special dignity and still brings a smile is the adjective---"bitchin." It's a fun word to pronounce, rolls easily off the tongue, and is uncontrived in tone. For proper enunciation, emphasis should be placed on the first syllable as in---*BITCH*in. The word has an almost Scandinavian tonal lilt. It was a positive word, used to describe something as intrinsically wonderful as in a bitchin sunset, or a bitchin looking girl.

Bitchin is a truly American word of unknown origin. More precisely, it is a southern, Southern California word with no known synonym and a word whose mastery requires a solid grasp of context acquired only by participant observation. To this day, modern etymology still gets it wrong by saying the word derives from "bitching" or complaining. A few sources correctly identify the word as part of surfer slang during the 1950s yet continue to misspell it as "bitchen" instead of bitchin.

Like most parents, my father sought desperately to communicate with his teenage son---a task he should have known was hopeless. Listening to my friends, pop was aware of the word "bitchin," yet couldn't quite get either its pronunciation or contextual usage correct.

Such ineptitude led him to say things like, "Hey, aren't those new Studebakers bitchy?" After several failed attempts to improve his linguistic skill, all tutoring ceased out of fear it would only encourage him. Knowing how these things go, I was only a sentence or two away from being assigned a new beach sobriquet: "Watch out, here comes bitchy brown."

Rarely is bitchin overheard today. Imagine, if you will, that paragon of the monosyllable---Donald Trump---declared during a press conference, "…my fellow Americans, I have some bitchin news." On second thought, I'm glad he stuck to his own manner of speaking so as not to sully a wonderful adjective.

WATERMAN ~ Although the word *"Waterman"* is daunting for folks who haven't grown up near an ocean, it is a vital component of this story. True enough, this noun is overheard more often today, but even as its awareness spreads, it fundamental meaning can remain elusive.

Perhaps the term's vagueness is due to its multiple origins. In some instances, the word can be traced as far back as the 11th century when English sailors made their living in small boats either as smugglers or fishermen. Only later did their American counterparts learn from Powhatan tribesmen how to make sturdy watercraft from loblolly pine and poplar trees. Distinguishing themselves as watermen, these hardy souls fished Chesapeake Bay, designing their work boats depending on function for crabbing, clamming, oystering, or line fishing. Still heard today is the dialect of those hearty and rugged Chesapeake watermen reflecting their respect for the sea, her moods and warnings.

Thousands of miles away, another version arose in the south Pacific where Polynesian Islanders, likely Tahiti, adopted deeper, almost mystical, tenets. For example, to become a waterman in *Kukui'ula* (southern Kauai), doesn't come easily because it is a title that must be earned. To be recognized as a waterman (or more recently as a waterwoman) one must master certain aquatic skills and also adopt the unique lifestyle of the sea.

Sometimes the expression *Kanaka Kahawai* can be heard, although it translates more as "river man." In other instances, *Kāne Kai* means a man of sea, but even then usage will vary regionally from one Polynesian locale to the next. Overall, the most descriptive Hawaiian word for waterman is *Kanaka Kai*---a way of life resting on five foundations. First, a waterman's knowledge is acquired from *'Ohana*, or the cumulative wisdom ancestors have passed down through generations via oral tradition; often by a family mentor. Next, the path of a waterman requires the mastery of skills as being a strong ocean swimmer, understanding currents, tides, weather, and the ocean's inhabitants. Additionally, he or she will know how to body or board surf perhaps augmented by kayaking, free diving, paddling, and lifeguarding. Equally important is knowing not only how to harvest the sea's abundance but also how to prepare and serve these treasures beyond merely barbequing store bought salmon from Costco. A related tradition is that true watermen will build their own tools rather than purchase them from a store or catalog.

Closer to home, the notion of "waterman" was first imported in the early 1920s and 30s. One of the more renown introductions to the Polynesian traditions was made by Duke Kahanamoku and George Freeth on the shores of southern California and even Ocean Beach. While their demonstrations brought out curious crowds, their efforts failed to enkindle widespread interest in watermanship.

Even today, most Californians tend to think of being a waterman in more practical and narrow terms. In other words, to be known as a waterman around the beaches of, say, San Diego, generally refers to a person who free dives for lobsters, is familiar with spearfishing, and is also a good body or board surfer yet tends to forego the more mystical aspects of the Polynesian way. While many local surfers might know the basics of, say, high and low tides, a waterman's understanding will extend further into, say, how neap and spring tides occur or how tidal periodicity can affect neck feeders and rip currents on sandy beaches.

In a word, being a waterman is not a rank, self-proclaimed title, or a fad; it is a lifestyle seeking to understand and be part of the very ocean from which we emerged millions of years ago. Sometimes the Hawaiian word *Lōkahi* is invoked to describe a waterman's outlook: a philosophy that stresses the unity and harmony between humanity and the sea.

In 2019, the world lost Mike Doyle, a champion surfer and waterman who lived by the code. Before he died, he wrote:

> *By the time I was fifteen I'd already accepted the old tradition of the watermen as my own, and I set about the long process of mastering each of the waterman's skills. The tradition of the waterman comes from Polynesia and is different from the tradition of the sailor. The waterman's skills include surfing, paddling, rowing, and rough-water swimming…I learned that watermen who came before me didn't just go*

to the dive shop or the surf shop and buy the latest thing on the rack. They designed their own boards, their own dive gear, and their own outrigger canoes. They were constantly thinking and experimenting with other watermen about ways to perfect their gear. Nobody knew then how a surfboard should be designed. The only way to find out what worked and what didn't was to try it."

Overall, what my cohorts and I learned from our elders, or *Kumu A'o*, was that happiness in life isn't achieved solely from the acquisition of material things, but rather comes from balancing the mind, body and wisdom that one can acquire from the temple of the sea and its priests. Even though this statement may sound like hokum, it is worth noting that three conditions existed in the *Cradle* during the 1950s that made it easier for our elders to guide us: first, beach habitués were fewer in number and tended to co-mingle without age discrimination; second, youngsters were more respectful and eager to accept guidance; and, lastly, our elders willingly assumed the role and responsibility of mentorship.

A. Lee Brown

LOCATION

WHEN WORLD WAR II ENDED, Americans took advantage of new mobility. Many headed West, and like Wildebeests migrating across the Serengeti Plain, my family joined that irresistible allure. In 1946, dad loaded us and our raggedy belongings into a tattered pre-war Plymouth and drove into the setting sun.

Laguna Beach, California was our first stop where pop got a job at the Pottery Shack; a local business still found on the Pacific Coast Highway. It was a low paying job with the benefit of allowing ample time to pursue his passion: beach

combing. His arms loaded with flotsam debris, my father would return to sculpt his treasures into artistic and decorative forms. His favorite, and most profitable creations, were called Ming Trees that he crafted from driftwood using a white, ground moss to resemble branches.

As a six-year-old, I was too young to comprehend how much my life would be affected by Lee and Athamae Brown's decision to move to California. Almost immediately, the first order of business became fending off playground bullies making fun of my Texas twang and mannerisms. After several shoving matches and a successful headlock, the hazers shifted to other new arrivals and my life began in earnest.

For me, those three years were nonpareil. I had the run of the town. Pals taught me how to cadge fresh vegetables from neighborhood gardens and sneak down to the beach at the foot of Brooks Street. Although it didn't snow at Christmas, Santa never failed to appear mysteriously in the middle of the night bearing treasures like an

American Flyer electric train, a Red Ryder BB Gun or a used, rickety red bicycle. Best of all, was the arrival of a moody fox-terrier as reward for enduring a tonsillectomy. Named Spot, the two of us became inseparable, free to explore the artsy community, wave hello to Betty Davis, Victor Mature and other Hollywood Stars. Pop even took part in the Laguna Beach playhouse with a speaking part in Jack Kirkland's dramatization of Mary Lasswell's 1942 novel, *Suds-In-Your-Eye*. Saturdays were often spent in the village's only movie theater where, for twenty-five cents, kids could watch Buster Crabbe thwart death rays from the planet Mongo or maybe see Hoppy, Roy, and Gene whup villains, all who seemed to be named Blackie.

One memorable New Year's Eve, pop brought home a bearded co-worker named Eiler Larsen. Being recent transplants, the Dane and the Texan decided to get shit-housed after work and, in the spirit of the holidays, Lee Sr. offered his new buddy shelter in our garage. The next morning, my mother's clarion shriek awoke the neighbors, having discovered what she was sure was a corpse in the Plymouth's back seat. To this day, I cannot drive past the Greeter's statute on Pacific Coast Highway without hearing that blood curdling scream.

In 1949, dad got a new job so we moved again, an hour's drive down the coast. Ocean Beach was an affordable coastal community where we landed in a small, three-bedroom, one bath, rental on Adair Street in sight of the Pacific Ocean---a few hundred yards westward.

Despite working hard their entire lives, my parents never made enough money to make ends meet. Mom worked as a bookkeeper for Blue Pacific Nursery while pop took whatever came his way. Once, he tried to go into business for himself, but no matter how many hours he devoted to that flower shop, it was never enough. Ultimately, the venture's failure destroyed not only what remained of his dwindling self-confidence, it also got him in trouble with the California Franchise Tax Board. As a result, mom's wages were promptly garnished virtually assuring dad's spiral into serious alcoholism. As the skies would darken, cheap whiskey would appear from multiple hidey-holes and for a few hours his life would become meaningful, happy, and gay.

When my sister was born, our Texas grandmother, Mammo, arrived to help, then stayed for a quarter century. There we were, five people existing in a 900 square foot dwelling with one bath. While close proximity nurtured domestic rancor, mom sought to mitigate the direness by harvesting San Diego's free gifts. Sunsets were spent on the front porch bidding farewell to the golden orb while listening to vinyl 78s. Anything that could be had on the cheap became her passion. Maybe it was mustard and mayonnaise sandwiches in Balboa Park followed by a carousel ride, or driving to Pasadena to see the Rose Parade. What really opened new windows for my sister and I was the purchase of a used, RCA 12 inch black and white television.

Both mom and Mammo loved to bet the nags and would spend hours poring over Agua Caliente racing forms then make $2 bets with a bookie in an OB magazine store. Although in her 70s, my grandmother would receive a new Texas driver's license each year mailed by her sons. My sister and I began to suspect it wasn't so much a gesture of family affection as an incentive for their mother to remain in California. Being the only licensed driver among her circle, Mammo would chauffeur a carload of blue-hairs to Tijuana to bet on the greyhounds. More often than not, she would get disoriented in coastal fog on the way home, where, my hard scrabble Texas grandmother would knock on some stranger's door while parked on his front lawn and ask to use the phone.

Always the dreamer, mom was convinced I was a dead ringer for Carl Switzer, better known as "Alfalfa," of the Little Rascal's comedy films. On a gamble, she saved enough money to hire some smarmy Hollywood agent who took her money, promising a future career with Hal Roach. The only tangible result was a Social Security card at age seven.

In 1952, my first real job came along. Up at four a.m. seven days a week, Spot would sit passively as I folded the *San Diego Union* then we'd head for work a mile away. The route included three parallel streets, each one terminating at the seashore. It was sensory overload. It didn't take long to appreciate the pungency of the sea's briny odor and its ensemble of murmurs. No matter how confused or angry I would get---as irritable, acne riddled, adolescents are prone to do---the serenity of the Pacific at dawn provided a balm of its own.

21

A. Lee Brown

My first occupation wasn't easy, engendering the onset of inevitable drowsiness during morning classes at Dana Junior High. Pedants quickly anointed me a listless dunderhead, a juvenile without ambition. My grades fell inversely to the rise of parent teacher conferences. On the upside, $30 a month helped at holidays; sadly, on more than one occasion, it also helped bail pop out of the cooler.

Our perennial worry was eviction, an event occurring more than I care to remember. Although not obvious at first, eventually it became clear that poverty had a predictable cycle. The poorer we were, the poorer we got, which, in turn, brought increasing dire consequences. The cycle usually began in mid-summer when my parents would first fall a little behind in rent. Over the next few months, the indebtedness would grow progressively worse, eventually leading to a Notice to Vacate: almost always at Christmas. Unlike a Dicken's tale, however, the ghost of Christmas Past never intervened to make things better. True enough, the holidays provided pop an opportunity to earn extra money by making corsages for corporate parties. It was also heart wrenching to see him out in that unheated garage with two bottles within reach: aspirin and booze; frequent doses of both helping to mute the acute pain of arthritic hands shaping festive bouquets.

A levity of sorts characterized our fiscal despair. All of the homes in that area had been built toward the end of War II by Palmer Construction using a standard floor plan. By some dispensation of providence, every time we were evicted from one Palmer house, Lee and Athamae would manage to find another. Then, like hermit crabs, the five of us would leave one boxlike domicile to enter another up the street. The bonus of "moving day," was knowing room assignments in advance, thereby reducing the leer time of curious neighbors.

For years, my sister shared a room with our grandmother, at least until Mammo's nightmares became intolerable. As a gesture of sibling goodwill, I offered my room to my sister and moved into the garage which, despite being colder, was at least beyond earshot from the house of nocturnal screams.

From 1950 to 1960, this is how we lived. Hand to mouth, a family fractured by frustration, alcoholism, and discord, yet all the while my parents remained anchored to the values of their own youth; aptly named by Tom Brokaw as the "Greatest Generation." No matter how bad it got, divorce was never mentioned, and the lesson passed along was that no one owes you anything. In short, better learn to hunker down, soldier on, and make the best of it. Or, as my mother was wont to say, "Whining isn't becoming." Taking her advice in stride, my personal escape became a pivot to the sea's intoxication, power and tranquility.

Ocean Beach, California is what I call the *"Cradle"* of my youth. Its geographic attributes remain as they were seventy years ago---a coastal village bordered on the north by a deep ocean channel allowing access to San Diego's sprawling seawater park known as Mission Bay. To the east and south lies the rest of Point Loma, and on OB's west is the magnificent Pacific Ocean. Overall, today it remains the same three-square miles of dwellings and commercial activity while having a larger population now closer to 30,000 people.

Fulfilling a promise to my grandson, we recently revisited my family's parade of former dwellings. It was surprising to see how much the Palmer homes had been remodeled to the point it was difficult to identify them. Not far away, where the historical Azure Vista military housing project once existed, are tony single-family homes, now worth millions.

Over the last century, OB evolved in fits and lurches. Its most notable early attempt at commercial development involved two men, Bill Carlson and Frank Higgins. In 1887, they acquired pueblo land rights hoping to subdivide and market their investment. Visited primarily by curious picnickers, their vision failed; even the extension of a trolley line didn't help. It seemed tourists were more enchanted with Coronado's tent city and its upscale new hotel. With their gamble failing, Higgins committed suicide. Even well into the 20th century, less than a hundred homes dotted the 2,000-acre OB landscape.

Subsequent ventures suffered similar fates. In 1913, two brothers took a swing at making OB a destination amusement center. Naming their project Wonderland, it extended from the "False Bay" of marsh and wetlands on the north to the southern terminus occupied by a saltwater plunge and water slide. Perhaps their most striking investment was the construction of the Blue Streak, the largest roller coaster on the west coast. Before long, more carnival attractions arrived including a dance hall, bowling alley, animal menagerie, carousel, and games of chance. Stupendous as these alternatives were, they could not sustain public interest as the gawkers tended to come only once then head for the growing allure of Balboa Park and the 1915 Panama Exposition.

A harbinger of the ocean's ferocity appeared the following winter when storms and king tides swept the coaster, and most of its neighbors, out to sea thus foreclosing another dream. And, all the while, with powerful obduracy, the Pacific Ocean continued to demonstrate its capacity to absorb and neutralize the best of humanity's challenges.

In the early 20th Century, few people swam in the surf, preferring to roll up pant cuffs and wade in foamy ankle-deep water. Ever wary of the treacherous sea, few "bathers" became swimmers---especially after a volunteer lifeguard drowned in 1906 attempting a rescue. In 1916, Hawaiian legends Duke Kahanamoku and George Freeth came to demonstrate stand-up surfing on boards and, while well-received, attracted very few converts.

World War II changed everything. During the first half of the 1940s a human conveyor belt shuffled military personnel and defense workers through town, many of whom decided to remain at war's end. San Diego's population soared from a pre-war base of less than 200,000 in 1940, to double that by 1950, and quadrupled by 1960. It proved to be an enormous boon for the Ocean Beach community as lovers of temperate climate formed a conga line of emigrants down the king palms lining Newport Avenue to the seashore.

LIQUID

O N FRIDAY, JUNE 19, 1959 (curiously the year of the Pig), two bizarre events took place. Governor Earl Long of Louisiana was put in an insane asylum and San Diego Unified Schools saw fit to release me from captivity. By another quirk of fate, two days later I was hired by the respected Scripps Institute of Oceanography.

Ever since, my occupational life has played out like a Bach fugue; a

rondo of jobs all revolving around two atoms of hydrogen and one of oxygen. For more than a half-century, my work-a-day world has been a series of aqueous associations beginning with Scripps, then a decade of ocean lifeguarding, a High Sierra ski patrolman, and later a professor of water resources. Interspersed in those years was time spent as Director of the U.S. Department of Energy's Institute for Water and Energy, and head of Idaho's Environmental Resources Center. In similar fashion, time was also spent with Texas Department of Water Resources, a field hydrologist for The Nature Conservancy, and regional manager for Idaho Water Engineering.

As teachers tell their pupils, water touches us in three forms: as a gas, liquid, or solid and I've been fondled by all three in the world's oceans, estuaries, snowfields, lakes, rivers, and irrigation canals. My early waterman days extended into a lifetime of aquatic immersion.

What I learned was that the science of hydrology rests upon a concept known as the "Hydrologic Cycle;" a view assuming there is a fixed amount of water that not only encircles the globe but is in constant motion. Each day the sun burns off trillions of gallons from the oceans, most of which fall as precipitation before reaching land. The rest moves ashore until it, too, drops to earth to begin its return to the sea.

Of course, there is more to this complex process which is why I like to think of water's cycle as a metaphor of life. At their high mountain birthplaces, brooks are like sprites; playful, and self-indulgent. Unfettered, they gurgle and bounce from rock to rock like mischievous nymphs in search of fun. In their unpolluted childhood, water scientists call such aquatic youngsters, "gaining streams." Why? Because, like selfish infants, they take what they can, indifferent to their neighbors and unaware of the journey to follow.

Acquiring confidence, brooks turn into creeks nourished by freshets and groundwater. Energized by gravity, they become robust and join their cousins to form streams which, in turn, become rivers. It is also at this stage where rivers enter a transitional zone and become larger, unpredictable, even dangerous.

Further downstream, things change again. The once robust flow begins to lose energy to its neighbors as vegetation, animals, and humans all compete for a river's life-giving properties. Like middle-aged men, rivers broaden at the waistline and begin to react more slowly. Approaching its destination, the once mighty river becomes braided, shallow, weak, and often polluted. No longer able to perform, this exhausted remnant seeks its destiny and rejoins the womb of Mother Earth; the very origin from which cyanobacteria first emerged a billion years ago.

Inherent within the hydrologic cycle is a waterman's most fundamental lessons. Life, too, is in constant flux and learning to deal with the unexpected is a valuable key to opening the door to personal happiness.

It is not by accident that all major civilizations are established on rivers or seaports (or both). Such proximity raises another question, do we live near water solely for commercial activity or is there a deeper connection? Only fools don't learn from their work, which is why I am convinced there is a closer bond between humanity and water than we realize. Afterall, life originates in mom's reservoir, where her fetus is cradled for thousands of hours in a watery amniotic environment. As adults, we are walking canteens. Our skin cells contain 60 percent water, blood is 90 percent, brains and muscles 75 percent, while blood and water share an identical pH balance.

With such biochemistry, it's easy to see why aquatic recreation is popular. When a person dives into a clear mountain stream or catches an ocean wave, is it recreation or "re"-creation? If religions use water to anoint believers and cleanse their souls, could it be that by immersion in Earth's "amniotic" gifts we feel purified and reborn? I know from a lifetime of being part of earth's natural waters it is both a whimsical and incommunicable experience.

A. Lee Brown

CRADLE'S CAMPUSES

T HANKFULLY, HOLLYWOOD HAS PROVIDED audiences
with a cornucopia of entertaining films; most of which are good,
a couple of stinkers, and many "tweeners." For my dough, a
memorable production was *Twelve O'clock High*; a film winning wide
acclaim including Dean Jagger's Oscar performance.
Director Henry King opened this film with the camera following
Jagger on his bicycle pedaling along a rural English lane to the entrance
of an abandoned World War II aerodrome. Leaning his bike against a
wooden gate, the retired airman crosses time's runway and becomes
transfixed with nostalgia and begins to hear sounds of throaty B-17
radial engines merging with long-gone music and voices.

Most likely, the opening scene strikes such a concordant note
because I, too, experience similar emotions whenever passing the
haunts of years gone by. Three places, in particular, are etched in
memory and woven deeply into the fabric of my personality. Taken as
a whole, these places structured my values and prioritized my interests
for the rest of my life. All are found on the western shore of Point
Loma, California.

Geographically, the southernmost unit of the Cradle is known as
Sunset Cliffs and stretches for about a mile from where I lived, down
to the terminus of Sunset Cliffs Boulevard. At that point, a staircase
descends to the Pacific Ocean. For surfers and divers this access is
Heaven's Gate, for curious beachcombers and tourists it becomes a
point beyond which they are reluctant to venture further to spelunk
the coves and caves below.

Moving north from the Cliffs, the middle section of the Cradle is
found at the terminus of Pescadero Avenue. Like the cliffs, this access
also leads to a sandy cove, albeit smaller, where surfing and diving takes
place.

And, lastly, the third, and most northern, component of the Cradle
is the village of Ocean Beach. It is where merchants, cafes, bars, and
shops align the three blocks of Newport Avenue down to a sea wall.
On the other side of the wall is where the sand meets the Pacific

Ocean. This community of Ocean Beach, or "OB," as it is known colloquially, is a popular surf spot despite its dangerous currents and conditions. Likewise, it is a hangout for colorful characters and transients within the watchful purview of the year-round lifeguard facility. For example, the two gentlemen in this photo were Jim Maroudis (left) and Clint Carey (right)---both well-known around Ocean Beach in earlier times.

Jim Maroudis was a harmless soul whose desire to be accepted often pushed him to the outer limits of absurdity. Part of his personae was true while much of his mystique had been fabricated by others. True enough, Jim was infatuated with electronics and television parts as evidenced by his vast collection of electronic junk and tv antennae amassed in his parent's back yard. Well aware of the City's schedule for trash days, he would make the rounds and retrieve as much as he could until his bicycle became so unstable, he'd have to stash his treasures then return to gather more.

It was often difficult to disentangle fact from fiction, but it was widely rumored Maroudis would experiment by planting his antennae then water them with oil. Even stranger, so it was said, that to keep her son from becoming disheartened, Mrs. Maroudis would tape on new pieces to make her son believe his garden was growing.

Well, who knows? I do know Jim used to scare the wits out of my mother which was my fault. Like most locals who befriended and protected Jim, he would download his "rescued" items at our house. My mother never ceased to marvel at the odd man stockpiling tv carnage behind her garage.

Carey was another source of OB's zany lore. This mildly deranged, alcoholic and diabetic man was a decent artist in the medium of ultra-violet painting. His nickname---OB Spaceman---was tied to his assertion he had once been visited by "Outer Space People" who told him they would be coming again. In anticipation of this visit he was ordered to provide free tickets to a select group of future passengers. I somehow remember mine as being XRB/2 although a friend's reserved flight was "X-King-D."

The Spaceman's favorite hangout was a bench near the intersection of Abbott and Newport---a place nicknamed the "Abbott Habit"--- where he was always assured a crowd. One brisk spring day he arrived with his wife known as Typewriter Woman. She would dutifully follow Carey on his rounds lugging an aging Remington. When a large enough crowd would collect, Carey would suddenly stop, turn to her, and shout, "Take a Letter!" He would then begin dictation usually addressed to LBJ, Richard Nixon, or Governor Moonbeam. With deft skill she would pound away at the keys punctuated by periodic carriage returns. Impressed with her skill, I once peeked over her shoulder only to see there was no paper on the roller carriage!

Taken together, the locations of Sunset Cliffs, Pescadero, and Ocean Beach, comport what I call my *Cradle* of Bitchin." Why so? Because during my youth, the curriculum of these three campuses was as important to my maturation and education as anything being taught in the classrooms of public schools---not better or worse but clearly different. Just as a student moves from an elementary school, through middle school, and high school, the campuses of the *Cradle* provided a sequential education producing watermen.

The Germans have a word describing the way of life during a particular time in history---*ZEITGEIST*. It's a good word, meaning something like, "spirit of the times." My childhood began to ebb in 1951, about the time I turned eleven. Compared to the previous decade, world turmoil was minimal except for the Korean War which was ill understood by children.

On the national political scene, America's leaders were chosen by alternating parties without disagreement as to voter outcomes. In fact, both presidents Truman and Eisenhower were respected men. At least, neither was the subject of impeachment. Sure, rumors of Ike's wartime dalliance with his Army driver, Kay Summersby, lingered, but even that disappeared with the end of WW II. All told, America was probably held in higher world esteem in 1946 than when John Winthrop first described the Massachusetts Bay Colony as a shining beacon for the world.

In the early 1950s, the US economy was vibrant having grown forty percent while un-employment was the lowest since WWII ended.

Inflation was minimal as American purchasing power tripled; likely due to balanced federal budgets. Manufacturing and home construction were booming, and into American living rooms once a week came Lucille Ball and Desi Arnaz with the most popular television series of all time---*I Love Lucy*.

Of course, the fifties were not immune to social disruptions and frightening occurrences. The Cold War was always imminent as the US and USSR vied with one another for arms and science, sending school kids under their desks in monthly atomic bomb drills. Illicit drugs were characterized simplistically as portrayed in the movie, *Reefer Madness*. Marijuana was thought to be an inconsequential issue fueled by organized crime and limited to certain cultural populations. Without a doubt, institutional racism was present. It was responsible for untold heartache in rural and urban America although its inhumanity had yet to acquire the political resources to move it to the forefront of social consciousness. The same could be said for inequities in women's rights and access to career marketplaces.

Conditions of awfulness did exist, although in our little insulated corner of the world, youngsters remained naïve and ignorant. Existentially speaking, we were dumb as stumps and only knew what we knew. In fact, living on Point Loma, our schools were racially integrated not by social justice, but as an artifact of large, nearby, military housing projects. As a white kid growing up in this milieu, I assumed our blend of races and religions was the same throughout the rest of the country. As a personal indication of the times, my parents never hesitated to allow a twelve-year-old to take the bus across town.

NURSERY SCHOOL ~ PESCADERO BEACH

All journeys have beginnings, and Pescadero Beach was my nursery; a place of discovery that opened the world of southern, Southern California's beach life.

As with most of San Diego's shoreline today, the terminus of Pescadero Avenue bears little resemblance to the redoubt it once provided for local youngsters. Six decades ago, this secluded sandy beach was a minor league hot spot for the cluster of boys and girls who gathered each summer. In 1952, my friend and neighbor, Ronnie Green, and I packed away our cap pistols, soap box derby entry forms and green plastic toy soldiers acquired with coupons from the back of comic books. Leaving childhood behind, our inaugural journey got underway; an odyssey in search of adventure which we found three blocks away.

At that age, Ron and I had no idea the word *pescado* meant "fish" in Spanish, or that a *pescadero* was a fishmonger. What we did know was that Pescadero Beach was a popular hangout for kids our age. Unknown to outsiders, it was a place rarely frequented by casual swimmers, parents, or similar rule enforcers. Its popularity inhered in its freedom and, as typical boys verging on teendom, we couldn't get enough. Kids clustered to smoke or gossip while listening to new devices called transistor radios playing the Chord's "Sha-Boom," or a new vocalist with a different jump named Little Richard screaming the "Taxi Blues" on the AM dial.

Access was easy; where Pescadero Avenue ended, a small drainage ravine led to the haven below. Once on the sand, beach towels were spread along the base of sandstone cliffs and despite the sea being but a few steps away, its waters were used primarily to cool off or perhaps, well, you know what.

Carrying inflated innertubes, Ronnie and I would sometimes venture north to OB to frolic under the watchful eyes of professional lifeguards. From where we played in the surf line, it was possible to watch the older beach boys paddle out on surfboards, catch a wave, then standup and ride back to shore. It was mesmerizing.

The only surfer I knew by name was Gordon Tribby, a big, red head, nicknamed Sunny. His parents lived on my paper route and we'd met a couple of times when I'd come to collect the monthly payment. Despite his intimidating size, Sunny was a pleasant fellow who had recently graduated from Point Loma High.

One day at OB, as he was coming out of the water, we recognized each other.

"Hey there young fellow, how's it going?" he asked.

"Aw ok, Sunny, mind if I ask a question?"

"Not at all, junior, what's on your mind"

"I've seen you surfing and wondered how you got started?"

Laughing out loud, Tribby responded, "I often ask myself that question. I guess it was when some older guys in the QWIIGS helped teach me a couple of years ago."

Like so many answers, this led me to another question, "I've seen those jackets around, what does it mean?"

"It was a surfing club started here at Point Loma High in 1938."

A. Lee Brown

What happened next changed my life forever.

"Say junior, I'm going in the Army at the end of this month and if you want to buy my board, I'll make you a deal"

It was as if I'd won the sweepstakes. "That'd be great, although I'm not sure I can pay for it; how much do you want?"

Tribby looked me over. "Here's where the deal comes in. You deliver the morning paper to my folks free for six months?"

We shook hands and that's how a life shaping adventure began. In many ways the deal worked out even better because when I told Ronnie he offered to split the work since he had the route next to mine. If I would deliver the morning paper to Tribby's parents for three months, he'd do the same.

Our agreement proved to be more than a financial one. The board was a ten-foot plank with rounded redwood rails and single stringer. Tribby said it had been shaped by Joe Quigg, an innovative and famous board maker in the late forties and early fifties. Later, I learned this was doubtful given its small rudder and rockerless plane. More likely it was modeled by the inventive surfer from La Jolla named Bob Simmons. He had been a Cal-tech graduate that drowned mysteriously on a foggy big surf day at Windansea beach.

Today, that board would be a collector's item on display in some upscale, svelte restaurant. It didn't take long for Ron and I to wonder if we'd gotten the short end of the deal. The board turned out to have the displacement of a frigate, at least sixty pounds. Truth be told, it was already obsolete as the new, lighter, balsa boards were beginning to appear, shaped by a fellow in Dana Point named Hobart Laidlaw Alter. Little did we care. The plank was ours and we were surfers.

Life is curious, isn't it? No matter what one has in mind, often the unanticipated takes over. Our board was so heavy it was like trying to launch the battleship Missouri. Fortunately, the problem was solved by the largesse of two fellows who, observing our dilemma, offered to keep the Titanic in their backyard adjacent to Pescadero beach.

The next problem wasn't as easy. Even floating in the water, the freighter was so heavy we weren't strong enough to paddle outside beyond breakers. Our dream of learning to ride swells was abandoned in favor of staying inside to catch the foam of already crested waves. Despite this concession, we remained hapless because neither of us had enough arm power to overcome inertia and get going fast enough to have the soup pick us up.

34

Witnessing our struggle, an older guy with enormous ears---named Dumbo---stepped in. Turned out our benefactor wasn't as simple minded as his nickname implied. In quick order, he showed us how to keep the board's nose pointed shoreward while wading out until in chest high water. When the foam of a crested wave would approach, Dumbo would steady the board so her crew could climb aboard then Ron and I would knee paddle furiously for the beach. Yes, we had our share of maritime mishaps, but with practice and determination ultimately Ron and I became adept at matching a broken wave's speed. Once we were "in" the wave's energy, the other would jump off so the rider could attempt to stand and balance into shore. The remainder of that first summer was spent attempting to improve a beginner's take off.

Ron and I were labeled "kooks" which didn't bother us because we were. Despite the disparaging nickname, it also meant we were on our way. No one is really sure of the exact origin of the word. Most likely it was a cousin of the Hawaiian adjective *kūkae,* or feces and was brought back by Gis returning from the South Pacific. In any event, it was a negative adjective referring to beginning surfers who not only lacked skills but were also ignorant of the most rudimentary elements of the surfer's code.

I had nearly forgotten the term until a few years ago standing at the foot of Kahauola Street on Oahu's northern shore, a zone better known as Banzai Beach. There, planted in the sand in front of the county lifeguard station, was a sign declaring, "NO KOOKS." It was a bit mean spirited but, given my own experience as an ocean lifeguard, it made me wish we'd had similar signs instead of warning flags.

Unfortunately, our discovery of Pescadero was a little too late. Just as we were beginning to be accepted by regulars, the ocean temperatures nosedived, and schools reopened. Ron returned to Sacred Heart Academy, and I was off to 6th grade at Silver Gate Elementary to meet a woman teacher I have worked ceaselessly to erase from memory. Later in life, I often had teachers as students in my own university courses hoping that one day the bitch from Buchenwald would appear---no luck.

The following summer was perhaps the most wonderful memory of all. In 1954, gasoline was thirty cents a gallon, new Fords cost $1,500 while the average annual gross income was less than $4,000. On an isolated atoll in the Marshall Islands, a dry fuel thermonuclear device was ignited called the Hydrogen bomb which, although terrifying, was of little consequence to our isolation on Pescadero Beach. Even more distant, France lost some battle named Dienbienphu; in those days I hardly knew where France was much less Vietnam. It was also when a British scientist named Francis Crick shared the Nobel Prize for discovering how DNA worked. I had no clue that decades later I would have lunch with him.

On the cultural side, *From Here to Eternity* got the Oscar despite my crowd's opinion it should have gone to Jack Arnold's, *Creature from the Black Lagoon*. Records were appearing on new 45 rpm disks playing songs like *Shake, Rattle and Roll* by Bill Hailey and the Comets. And in literature, Ernest Hemingway walked away with the Nobel Prize in Literature as a lesser-known writer, William Golding, was just beginning his masterpiece, *Lord of the Flies* for which he, too, would later receive the same accolade.

As we frolicked in the ocean, Rocco Francis Marchegiano, aka Rocky Marciano, continued his reign in boxing as did San Diego's light heavy weight champion---the Mongoose---Archie Moore. The New York Giants took the World Series with Willie Mays making the most famous catch in baseball history. Roger Bannister ran the first sub-four-minute mile, and the Cleveland Browns smushed the Detroit Lions for the NFL championship. In government, the US Supreme Court ruled---in <u>Brown vs. Topeka</u>---that segregated schools can never be equal while the U.S. House of Representatives KO'ed the communist hysteria of Congressman Joe McCarthy via a public censure.

More important to us was Dumbo's return and resumption of his role as mentor in elementary watermanship. We learned the Pacific Ocean is a mixed semi-diurnal tidal system having two highs and two lows with arrival times advancing about fifty minutes every twelve hours. We learned that "rip" currents (not "rip" tides) are formed differently on sandy beaches than rocky ones. Every day brought a new lesson on wave formation, ocean salinity, and what makes red tides luminescent.

Two older fellows, Ray and Barney, allowed us to tend their innertubes with attached gunny sacks to hold green abalones found along the outer reef. By sharing a glass face mask, Ron and I could watch them pry gastropods off the submerged rocks using metal tire irons. At first, these clamping creatures looked yucky, yet, when prepared and served, it was instantly clear why this delicacy was so cherished. In similar fashion, the nursery faculty introduced us to spear fishing for halibut and how to hoop net for corbina. The allure of the sea was just beginning to make her treasures irresistible.

The summer of 1954 also provided initial lessons of the surfer's ethical code (seemingly repealed today) of sharing waves and respect; courtesies that are especially important for safety in large surf where mishaps can result in serious injury.

Eventually, Ron and I were able to balance upright long enough to catch short rides to the beach, although attempts to maneuver or turn by dragging a foot remained futile. Life improved when an older, and wealthier, kid named Mel let me try his new balsa Hobie. The difference was indescribable. Small and light, I could paddle the board outside to actually catch waves off the Pescadero reef. Tippy at first, a fundamental grasp of how to turn eventually arrived—at least going to the right. In the meantime, Ronnie had acquired his own board. It was one of the strangest looking, spoon billed, homemade surfboards ever made. It didn't matter, with his Joe E. Brown elastic smile, he'd don a Papale palm frond Hawaiian hat and stay in the water for hours.

That summer provided one of life's most wonderful times. It could have been made better only by having a steady girl, possessing a driver's license, and less domestic conflict at home. When it ended, the beach gang again dispersed. Reluctant to give it up, a few of us clung to gathering on weekends.

One fall morning, Ron, Bob Mulrooney, and I found three unopened cans of Country Club Stout Malt Liquor leftover from a sailors' party the night before. Unable to open our treasure, we hid the small cans in the sand and returned at dusk armed with a church key singing a chorus like the crew of the Walrus, "*Yo ho ho and a bottle of rum, fifteen men on a dead man's chest.*" Of course, the lyrics were incorrect, but it didn't matter; at that moment we were pirates on the edge of adventure and verging on the edge of a beach boy bar mitzvah. We stood with one foot in childhood and the other in adolescence, not grasping where we had been, unable to see where we were going. Having never experienced alcohol, the pleasant and mysterious effect swept us away until we unclothed and ran into the sea in a feeble effort to purify our transgression.

Ronnie and I remained pals for a long, long time. Thirty-two years later, Bob and I were his pall bearers, a sad and premature death under shadowy circumstances took him away. Even so, the summer of 1954 was an initiation into the world of rudimentary watermanship, and I was addicted.

Eventually, the glory of that summer began to ebb, replaced by a hint of fall. Autumn arrives in San Diego not so much with a flourish but subtlety as schools open and ocean temperatures drop thus heralding the closing of Pescadero's nursery. As fall thickened into winter, the nursery scattered. Ron and Mulrooney again returned to Sacred Heart Academy in OB as I headed over the hill to Dana Jr. High. At first, it was a life-threatening situation, being compelled to deal with a completely new environment. My school bus originated in the Azure Vista housing project and by the time it arrived at my stop was already occupied with a mix of older kids and cigarette smoking badasses eager to bully somebody. My *bête noire* was Beverly Arias, nicknamed "Apache Woman," a tough chick who seemed determined to torment me.

On the second day of beginning band, the teacher received a note calling him to the office and, to my horror, he handed me his baton and put me in charge to keep the "peace." No sooner had he departed than my wafer-thin authority was challenged by a kid from OB named Billy Jackson. When il maestro returned, Jackson and I were busy rolling through the trombones, scattering sheet music like a ticker tape parade on Wall Street. In short order, both combatants were sent to the principal's office and parents notified to come get us. It was an event confirming my mother's suspicion I was destined to be a juvenile delinquent, in school two days and already in trouble.

School conflicts aside, 1954 was wonderful. Pescadero's nursery had helped self-confidence which made it easier to deal with acne and similar challenges. Ron and I agreed, it was time to move to the next level---Ocean Beach.

My last, and regrettably, most memorable encounter with Pescadero took place years later while working as a lifeguard for the City of San Diego. On Lincoln's Birthday in 1962, HQ notified us about a Code 3 incident at Pescadero. It was a chilly midwinter morning and other units were already on scene when we arrived. Not knowing what to expect, I grabbed the resuscitator and ran past the small crowd of gawkers being restrained by police to the beach below.

Suddenly it all made sense. Torrential rain the previous night had weakened the sandstone roof of their cave burying three young boys.

Other guards and firemen were digging frantically to pull them from nature's grasp. Until that moment, I had only seen corpses on television, but seeing their frozen, inanimate faces, one of whom I knew, was paralytic. Efforts to clear sand from their glazed eyes and open mouths was fruitless and as Bob Cosgrove, a senior guard, moved from one victim to the next his expression told it all. When the ambulance crew arrived, I overhead Bob murmur the brevity code 11-44 for "coroner's case." Over my decade of service, those numbers would be repeated all too often.

That day was my first encounter with death; demonstrable evidence of the immutable laws of nature; statutes we ignore only at great peril. Rules that apply to all and ignorance provides no immunity.

MIDDLE SCHOOL ~ OCEAN BEACH

In Ocean Beach, where Santa Monica Street terminates at the Pacific Ocean, there is a permanent lifeguard facility presiding over its domain. Practical and not without purpose, this building bears little resemblance to what was once a shrine. In the 1950s, the entire area was about the size of a college basketball court. Despite its ramshackle appearance, it was the centerpiece of our lives---a place that was the core of our existence and molded us forever.

The rosy colored stucco lifeguard tower was a redo of old police and fire substation. A few steps away, to the north, were remnants of the former Wonderland carousel where prancing giraffes and zebras once made their endless circuits. In the early fifties, Noel's furniture, bought the dilapidated building as a storage warehouse.

Adjacent to Noel's, an overhead sign proclaimed May's Burger Bar where beach goers placed their orders with the slender and often besotted May. Drunk or sober, she always had a Camel cigarette hanging from her mouth while flipping burgers for thirty cents. Directly across the lifeguard station's driveway, another eatery served similar fare. Known as the Cubby Hole, it was run by the Millers, a pair of affable women, middle-aged Jewish twins who spoke English with an accent of unknown origin.

It wasn't uncommon for May and the Miller sisters to engage in open economic competition that would sometimes get so heated the lifeguards were called to intervene.

In the early 1960s, May sold out to a woman named Nancy who's business acumen led her to relocate the kitchen to the eastern end of the former carousel building. The modification not only allowed the creation of a window where orders could be taken on Abbot Street, but a space for an outdoor Wurlitzer Bubbler juke box. It was pure genius. The machine pumped out Bobby Day's irresistible *Rockin Robin* attracting teens like pollen nectar does honeybees. Not long after, the Miller's sold to another OB character named Speedy Norton who promptly introduced his own menu of haute cuisine: frozen fudge bars, dill pickles, hot dogs and lots of sand fleas.

Two more structures rounded out this tight knit complex. Immediately behind Speedy's Cubby Hole was a shack with a couple beds and a few steps further, toward the ocean, was a small beach cottage. More stylish than the shack, the cottage provided shelter for assorted beach boys and permanent lifeguards. Its primary resident was Bob Baxley, the hirsute, barrel-chested head guard. Although no one called him "Bwana Bob" to his face, his nickname was apt; at least in his own estimation. And while he agitated many locals, Bob was---without doubt---a spectacular waterman. The same can be said for his roommate, Don Mellon. Both men were military veterans, one in the Air Force the other an Army paratrooper.

During the cottage's zenith it was homebase for a variety of characters including Chief of Lifeguards, Chuck Hardy. At one point Baxley was dating the young Swedish starlet May Britt, who achieved notoriety for her appearance in the Marlon Brandon film, *The Young Lions*. Bwana had invited her to the cottage to partake in one of his sumptuous dinners served in Hawaiian luau fashion. Unbeknownst to Baxley, however, another beach boy was selling tickets to a ladder where kids my age could try to peep her in the shower. A year later, Britt married Sammy Davis Jr., taking her career in another direction.

When winter would set in, a telephone line was strung from the main tower to the cottage so lunches and games could continue and the guards could still answer the emergency phone. Both veterans parlayed their ingenuity into careers. Don became a very a successful commercial real estate developer and Bwana a Superior Court judge.

Author, Ron Oldham, & Dick Arnold (1994)

On the ocean side of the tower, two small depressions were known as the "Polio Pools," their only source of replenishment being high tides. In the 1950s, however, the Army Corps of Engineers began dredging Mission Bay's entry channel and piping the extracted sand south for dispersion along OB's shoreline. Even though it enhanced the beach, there was an unintended consequence, it made a near perfect spot in front of the tower to spread towels and mingle. Ocean Beach's habitués were not segregated by age allowing younger surfers to interact with their elders on a respectful but friendly basis.

At that time, we ranged from about 14 to 15 years of age and my cohorts consisted of Bob McLean, Richard Arnold, Bill Clamp, Jerry Hembury, Tom Johnston and Ronnie Oldham. Like myself, a couple of these fellows had apprenticed at Pescadero; others got a head start by volunteering as junior guards at Ocean Beach.

What stitched us together was not just being in the same grade level throughout a decade, but the shared desire to become watermen. As is often the case, a ritual of hazing had to be endured. Aspiring kooks were expected to run errands, suffer the indignity of jokes, and endure impromptu physical discomforts known as pink bellies. This ritual was conducted by holding the victim on his back while the bare tummy was spanked until it turned pink. Speaking of the code, senior beach boys placed limits on bullying. My first encounter with the seriousness of this unwritten rule was watching an older guy named Gary administer an overzealous pink belly to a kid at least ten years his junior. When it was obvious Gary's glee had breached the limit, one of his own peers, Mike Considine, intervened, slapped him, while admonishing Gary, to "pick on someone your own size." This judicial act of protection not only widened the eyes of the Dominican inquisitor (who later apologized), but for the rest of us as well.

From the summer of 1955 on, Ocean Beach and Sunset Cliffs continued to become the center of my universe. It's difficult to recount all the events that occurred at that shrine except to say it was our sanctuary; a breeding ground of capers, events, jokes, contests, summer loves, acts of heroism, lessons, inventions, and sacrifice. It was a place to learn of good and evil, and it shaped our personalities.

Of course, there were competing activities, each demanding its own tithe for school, prep sports, family, and part-time jobs. Nonetheless-

--and this cannot be over stated---despite the fact that very few physical remnants of the *Cradle* remain, it was this very temple of connectivity that created a lifelong brotherhood of experiences shaping our values, ethics, and personalities for the rest of our lives. In this photo, are men who have known one another for over six decades including: a CPA, concert pianist and computer guru, two fire captains, an artist, airline pilot, water scientist, surfboard designer, former lifeguards, contractors, a superior court judge, and a free-spirited import/export merchant.

In 1980, my fortieth birthday bore witness to the demolition of the old Ocean Beach lifeguard tower to make room for a new rescue facility and paved parking lot. Quashed mercilessly, the timbers of May's Burgers, Nancy's juke box, Speedy Norton's Cubby Hole, Baxley's cottage, and the old carousel were hauled away unceremoniously. The key physical elements upon which the *Cradle* rested were all vanquished in the name of development. Today, this hallowed locale is inhabited by characters drawn from different origins, ages, and interests, wholly oblivious to what was once the "Abbot Habit."

FINISHING SCHOOL ~ SUNSET CLIFFS

The *Cradle's* third and final campus was a stretch of coastline along the western side of Point Loma. Geologically, the "Cliffs" are composed of soft, crumbling, sandstone known as the Bay Point formation deposited a hundred thousand years ago. Offshore are shallow marine reefs of sand and carbonate creating the surfing breaks known as Osprey Point, No Surf, and a rare winter break named Indicator to the north. Further to the south are similar surfing spots of Chasm, New Break, Ab, Sub, and Garbage.

The intersection of Sunset Cliffs Boulevard and Ladera Street is a focal point as surfers and onlookers of all ages, residences, and sexes still congregate. In yesteryear, it was also a balcony for a handful of people; all of whom had gone to Point Loma High and knew each other intimately. For this reason alone, I cannot drive past this intersection without sharing a whiff of Odysseus and his inability to resist the allure of Anthemoessa's Sirens. On a recent visit, I drove by a small group of long-term friends looking like evangelical revivalists waiting for worship to begin. All in their seventies or older, each man enjoying the sea's special *eau de toilette.*

More interesting is that this ritual has not been created solely by location and time. If asked, "why are you here?" the likely answer would be to discuss sports, argue politics, or maybe the stock market. Truth be told, the origin of this ceremonial rendezvous is habitual; something deeper than swapping stories while watching Pacific rollers break over distant reefs. Seeds of this ritual were planted in the rich loam of deep friendship and shared constancy. As the morning wanes, these fellows will disperse with a reluctant shrug and drift toward jobs, or sundry family chores. A few will wax up and paddle out.

In the 1950s, Sunset Cliffs was akin to the once famous Stevens finishing school for young girls except instead of learning posture by balancing books on our heads, we were taught the ways of the ocean.

By and large, it was a popular place for grown men, but over time acceptance was extended to young boys and girls. Linda Benson, for example, was a sophomore at Point Loma High in 1959. She earned respect by demonstrating her mastery of surfing skills winning both the women's West Coast Championship and later the Makaha International contest.

The primary spot for surfing was a break named "Ab," because the reef below produced green abalones. Access to the reef was via a dirt road off Ladera Street that was protected by a locked gate where only members of Sunset Cliffs Surf Club had keys---a very prized possession.

Sunset Cliffs was a favorite spot because in big winter surf it was a

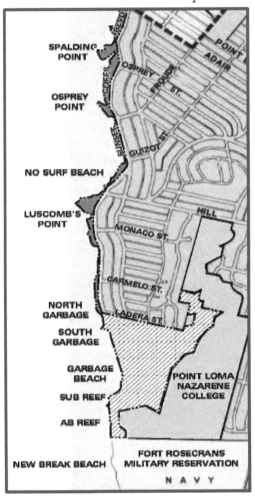

consistent break where waves were makeable. Ab was a left takeoff while Garbage and, later, New Break were better for regular stance surfers going right. As a rule, unproven surfers were sent to Sub which was an easier break between Ab and Garbage where they could practice until accepted by older beach boys.

Without a doubt, beyond that locked gate could have been a place for lawless mayhem; yet it wasn't. We were taught the surfer's code indirectly by observation and trial and error from a faculty that wasn't reluctant to discipline---just not physically. It was a place where cars were left unlocked and surfboards stayed overnight without fear of theft. While few words can fully describe the relationship between mentors and neophytes, it was like big brothers and their apprentices.

Nowadays, it's fashionable to point out the paradox existing between California's early beach ethic and its transformation into modern commercialism. I have no quarrel with critics who contend the original lifestyle of the *Cradle* was co-opted by the marketplace. Indeed, there is a great deal of truth in thinking the ways of earlier times are but quaint anachronisms. Only the most naïve would dispute the waterman ethics of the 1950s and early 1960s are now but distant ancestors of the financially successful industries who have harvested

44

the lore of the beach.

A. Lee Brown

OCEAN BEACH ~ CRADLE OF BITCHIN
(COURTESY OF DON MELLON)

PART II ~ *BEACH LIFE*

Oi kau ka lau, e hana I ola honua

Live your life while the sun is shining

A. Lee Brown

NEW HORIZONS

A ROUND THE TIME I TURNED FIFTEEN, life began to change. Until then, my world had been limited to family, school, and sports, along with trying to learn how to surf. By the mid-1950s, new portals and destinations were appearing.

UP THE COAST ~ Near summer's end in 1955, Richard Arnold opened the door to a new world. Dick had spent that summer volunteering as a junior lifeguard at Ocean Beach, an apprenticeship allowing him entry into the tight circle of older lifeguards and beachboys. It was one of their traditions to celebrate the passing of summer by spending a weekend camping and surfing up the coast. Dick had earned his invitation by merit and somehow had wrangled permission for me to tag along. It was a gesture that not only changed my life, it cemented our lifelong friendship.

Too young to drive, yet dying to take part in the ritual, it would have been disastrous if my parents had forbidden me to go. They didn't. Making things even better, Richard and I were assigned to accompany two men held in esteem as lords of the *Cradle*: Bud Caldwell and Marsh Malcolm.

North of Ocean Beach are other outstanding places to enjoy the ocean. Among these beaches are La Jolla, Encinitas, and Oceanside, yet my virgin excursion up the coast was to San Onofre. For millennia, this locale had been the site of an ancient village named *Panhe*, situated on the lands of the Acjachemen tribe. Although it is now a state park, for centuries its native inhabitants reaped the bounty of the freshwater marshes and offshore ocean kelp beds where San Mateo Creek discharges into the Pacific Ocean.

Meeting at the OB lifeguard tower, Richard introduced me to Bud and Marsh and the caravan got underway. A little over an hour later, we were setting up camp which didn't take long since all other participants had done this before. Then it was time for fun, and into the 70° ocean we went. As the youngest members, Bob McLean, Bill Clamp, Richard, and I were relegated to surf the gentle rolling breaks of Old Mans and Dogpatch leaving the experienced surfers to walk north to the waves of Trestles and Church.

After a few hours of desperate paddling, wobbly attempts to stand erect, and retrieving lost boards, we were exhausted and happy. Next, the stronger swimmers went spearfishing in the offshore kelp beds for halibut, calico bass, and maybe a sheepshead. As apprentices, we  assisted the divers going for abalone under reef shelves or lobsters hiding in the eel grass. That evening it all came together; hanging out with guys twice my age who were playing the music of Gabby Pahinui on ukuleles. At dusk, campfire cooks provided a sumptuous meal comprised of the day's catch along with steamed Pacific littleneck clams, butter scallops, and fresh salad served in a cardboard box.

An overwhelmed rookie, I hadn't anticipated Richard's prank inviting me to eat the small octopus he had boiled in a Maxwell coffee can. Not only did I feel sorry for the *cephalopod,* it was like chewing an inner tube. The next day I learned this menu had been "cooked up" as an initiation rite for my first up-the-coast adventure.

San Onofre captured me. Sunshine, warm ocean breezes and mixing freely with tender and encouraging teachers. It was a cosmopolitan place where surfers from further north began arriving and were welcomed as brothers. This was how I met other well-respected watermen as Loren "Whitey" Harrison and Don Okey.

That fall I had signed up to play sophomore football for Point Loma High. As luck would have it, two weeks into the season I broke a finger bone in my right hand during practice. The family physician determined it was a clean partial fracture and, after making a plaster cast, told me the gridiron was out for the rest of the season.

As it turned out, that mishap had a beneficial component because winter surf was beckoning. To protect the cast while surfing, several plastic bags were taped around the wrist yet despite this precaution the waterproofing didn't work. When it came time for the family doctor to evaluate how the broken digit was knitting, he opened the plaster cast only to discover sand and seaweed. Not only had my football future been suspended, now all water immersion got 86'ed as well.

As my generation began turning sixteen, the gateway to freedom materialized---legalized driving. North of the *Cradle,* the closest surfing beaches were Mission and Pacific Beach, PB Point and then La Jolla. Doubtlessly, the primary attraction was six miles further north at

Windansea with its famous "shack" and notorious surfers, big soft sand, and trickier and faster break.

In those days a unique and competitive relationship existed between the coastal communities of La Jolla and the *Cradle*. To understand the underlying dynamic of this association requires more than a brief comparison of reefs and breaks. Perhaps the simplest way to grasp these differences is to drive down Girard Avenue in La Jolla then make a similar patrol down Newport Avenue to the OB seawall. The dissimilarities are not subtle.

Let me risk a crude generalization. On one hand, many La Jollans envision themselves as an enclave, a very different cultural entity having little in common with the rest of San Diego. At the other extreme are Ocean Beacheans, who likely don't even conceptualize themselves in such civic terms. Whether the criterion for comparison is width of streets, personal income, number of art galleries or realtors per acre, it's easy to conclude a vast socio-economic and cultural chasm exists between these two coastal communities: both of which are within the city limits of San Diego.

In parallel fashion, comparing the way of life and personalities of the two beaches in the 1950s and early 1960s is a bit simplistic. From a distance, the general view was that Windansea drew more radical, cultured, and inventive daring doers. After all, Thomas Wolfe wrote an essay in his book about the "Pump House Gang" of La Jolla (despite Windansea locals calling him a foppish dork).

Often overlooked was the cross pollination between habitués of Windansea and Ocean Beach. Having grown up in the *Cradle* then spending years lifeguarding in La Jolla, I came to the conclusion they had more in common than either realized. Each shared an unequivocal love of the sea as a poultice to heal what was increasingly viewed as a world going awry. Both denizens shared a rejection of and retreat from conventional hierarchies and values. Take, for example, the following two photos snapped about the same time. One captures well-known surfers from Windansea, the other my cohorts from OB. Their poses were spontaneous and illustrative of their similarities.

Of the two beaches, Windansea was, and remains, more well-known both in and out of San Diego County. It came as no surprise in 1963 that the Beach Boys smash hit, "Surfin' U.S.A," included lyrics about La Jolla while snubbing Ocean Beach. Yet, on the other side, the 3rd World Championships were held at OB in 1966.

A. Lee Brown

But in the mid-20th century, a low-level magnetism was at work; an energy where opposing forces both attract and repulse. Eventually, the

connection between Point Loma and La Jolla settled down to a tolerable approach-avoidance link surfacing primarily with athletic events since both schools viewed each other as crosstown rivals.

Nicknamed "Take Me Out to the Brawl" game, the two schools  always met on the last day of the football season to decide who would capture the Bronze Shoe trophy. In the fall of 1958, the Pointers beat the Vikings triggering a bench-clearing melee that simmered for a long time. A year or so later, the two acknowledged bad asses from each school met at a party in Del Mar. The *Cradle's* slugger, Jack Pringle, KO'ed La Jollan Butch Van Artsdalen; some say affecting him for the rest of his soon to be shortened life.

On the whole, surfers from La Jolla and the *Cradle* tended to be indifferent to localism and it wasn't uncommon for us to surf at the notoriously protective Windansea or have La Jolla guys come our way.

On a personal level, I enjoyed playing bridge with Bill Kemp and his mother, surfing at Windansea, and knowing La Jollans like Art Perez, Bill Graham, Butch Van Artsdalen, P.G. Bent, Mike Diffenderfer and Bob Wineteer.

On occasion, crosstown friendships could get too close. In late summer of 1960, a mixed bunch from La Jolla and the *Cradle* went down to a bullfight in the new Plaza de Monumental de Playas. It goes without saying, alcohol was always the engine that drove reckless behavior. On that particular afternoon, I had decided to avoid alcohol and likewise, hopefully, trouble. About half-way through the first corrida, a Matador entered the ring to attract the bull's attention away from the picador and his horse. As he began executing his *quites,* or cape passes, an inebriated surfer from up the coast with long blonde hair stood across from us and threw half a watermelon into the ring. His aim missed the bullfighter, nonetheless, the federales grabbed the besotted gringo and whisked him out of sight.

Butch, sitting next to me, always the fearless champion of beach buddies (even ones he didn't know), grabbed me saying, "C'mon Brownie, let's rescue that guy." Not wanting to appear "hairless," I agreed, and we descended into the bullring's lower caverns where, sure enough, the federales were having their way with the belligerent offender. Without hesitation, and before I could dissuade him---no one "reasoned" with Butch when he had been drinking---Mr. Pipeline jumped into the fray and was immediately handcuffed and joined watermelon man on the way to TJ's notorious hoosegow. Alone and surrounded by a mob angry with Americanos in general, I faded into the crowd.

Van Artsdalen was eventually liberated by his La Jolla comrades. It was also the last time I went to a bullfight. Despite the color, music, and pageantry, I had come to realize those events tended to have as much finesse as when my dog was run over by a Pontiac.

Other similarities existed between Windansea and the *Cradle.* One was a shared infatuation with destroying old cars. Sometimes barely operable vehicles were mushed into each other at intersections like a destruction derby. In other instances, shorts were pushed over cliffs, or maybe---always a favorite---ignited.

Likewise, both groups would occasionally adorn German uniforms and ride Flexy Flyers to saltwater via storm drains. For La Jollans it was from Bonair to the ocean while the *Cradle's* pilots entered near the Food Basket on Catalina Blvd. down to San Diego Harbor. The

primary difference seemed to be the Windansea guys managed to catch rides on 8 mm film while the lads from OB didn't have cameras.

Whose antics were crazier? No one knows and, today, even fewer care. What was obvious was that La Jolla's escapades received more notoriety. Two incidents, in particular, were true products only of Windansea: Fleet Nelson keeping rattlesnakes in his car to prevent theft and Tiny Brain Thomas driving Billy Graham's car into the shore break to create a new surfing reef. Perhaps the closest similar event was when Bob Baxley drove a golf cart through the front door of OB's Arizona bar; a fit so tight it had to be partly dismantled to remove.

One of the most bizarre creations ever to come out of OB were nocturnal visits to the County Psychiatric Ward. Located in Hillcrest not far from Mercy Hospital, this escapade possessed all the right ingredients: originality, naughtiness, and a whiff of scarytown. Sorties typically involved foursomes and began after dark. Parking on a nearby street, we'd sneak down to the back windows and hoist the girls to look inside---usually at nothing. This form of beach humor ended abruptly the night I boosted my future wife up only to have another pair of eyes on the inside meet hers.

In the heyday of surfer's pranks, it was almost as if a long wire was stretched from Neptune Place to Newport Avenue thus connecting two empty tin cans like telephones. To the south of the *Cradle* were beaches of Coronado and Imperial Beach. For reasons I never understood, we had little interaction with beach people or surfers from those locations. With one exception---the waves of Tijuana Sloughs. Darkly repeated tales of the far outside breaks were scary.

The incorporated city of Imperial Beach is six miles south of San Diego where it touches the international border with Mexico. Separating the two countries is the Tijuana River, draining 1,700 square miles of headwaters mostly in Mexico. Where the river discharges into an intertidal coastal estuary, are three successive reefs. Geologists explain that the existence of these reefs is associated with the last glacial period ending some 15,000 years ago. As ice reservoirs receded, huge chunks of granitic rock were embedded in the floating ice, carried offshore, then deposited as the ice melted. As a result, when strong northern winter storm swells encounter the reefs, monster waves at short intervals are formed. A mile seaward is the furthest reef to the west known as the "Mystery Break," and this is where big surf is found.

At the end of World War II, early surfers like Bob "Goldie" Goldsmith, Woody Ekstrom, Buddy Hull, Skeeter Malcolm, and John Blakenship braved massive waves in frigid water a long ways away from safety. The undisputed master of the sloughs, however, was the Imperial Beach Lifeguard Allen Dempsey Holder.

As a young man, I had only heard of this austere place and finally mustered the courage to give it a try. At that time (1964), I was probably in the best physical condition of my life, swimming daily in cold winter water of La Jolla Cove. Even so, the thought of a solo venture to explore the rumored Mystery Break made me very, very nervous. Sitting in the safety of my old Ford and looking westward beyond the choppy, wind-blown, blue-grey seas there appeared to be white water on the horizon. "Yes," I reasoned with myself, "the Sloughs might be breaking way out there." After a small internal debate with myself about "hair," I smiled, drove back to IB for breakfast in a small café, and read the morning paper.

Up the Coast ~As experience and skill brought new courage, we turned to venturing further north. Halfway between San Diego and Los Angeles, is San Clemente State Beach, a convenient first night destination especially since our departure couldn't commence until after school ended on Fridays. Always economically stressed, it was necessary to either sleep uncomfortably in the cars or find some alternative spot.

Although no one knows who created this plan, the state park at San Clemente became a destination. Departing the *Cradle* after school on Fridays usually gave us time to buy a burger and wait outside the Park's boundaries until employees were gone and campers were snoozing. Creeping into the park we'd spread sleeping bags on the floor of the men's public rest room. Although it wasn't the Travel Lodge, the price was right.

That scheme served as a working option until it didn't! Somewhere around two in the morning Ton Chatto and Terry Bowman sensed tiny feet scurrying in their sleeping bags, a discovery that aroused fellow squatters. Contagion spread quickly as a flashlight verified small spiders accompanied by hordes of piss ants were coming from the urinals. Unable to neutralize the invasion, our free lodge was abandoned. Bug ridden sleeping bags were left outside our cars as we tried, in vain, to sleep sitting up. The rest of the night passed slowly, plagued with imaginary itches and renewed determination to seek a different accommodation in the future.

Eventually, dawn arrived allowing the disheveled convoy to assemble and drive on to Laguna Beach. Drowsy and scruffy, everyone but me opted for breakfast while I paddled out at the foot of Brooks Street for old time's sake. Although the waves were small, at least the cold sea washed away the urge to scratch.

Several similar ventures up the coast were met with moderate success. Once, while I still had a Ford Woody wagon, Bill Clamp, Tony Chatto, Dave Willingham and I headed north up the Pacific Coast Highway. Our first stop was Lunada Bay on Palos Verdes point. Picturesque in vista, the surf was flat plus it had a reputation for local rich kids harassing newcomers. We kept going.

Conditions at Redondo Beach, King Harbor, and Hermosa Beach were no better, generating a discussion as to whether to admit defeat and head for home. Mulling over alternatives, Billy Clamp remembered it was here, at the Hermosa Biltmore Hotel, that Dewey Weber worked as a lifeguard. Bill had met the legendary surfer once at Velzy's and suggested we look him up. "He's a good guy to know." Since Clamp was likewise an emerging Prince of the Beach, his suggestion was readily accepted.

For me, Bill's idea was solid, albeit for an entirely different reason. Sure, Weber's style and mastery of surfing had earned a reputation as

not only a surfer but leader in surfboard design. Additionally, Dewey was an excellent athlete having won the CIF wrestling crown while at Mira Costa High in his weight division (5' 3" and 138 pounds). Why I wanted to meet him, however, had nothing to do with any of his other laurels. He had dominated the national Duncan Yo-Yo competitions for three consecutive years.

Alas, the rest of the day was frittered away chasing bogus tips by locals as to Weber's whereabouts, which, we came to suspect, were being offered at our expense. With dark approaching, the focus shifted to finding a "benefactor" and a place to sleep. The benefactor arrived as an old wino who bought us a gallon of Red Mountain vin rose plus a bottle of Thunderbird for himself.

Fortified, the search began in earnest for local surfers willing to let us crash at their cribs for the night. With Billy as observer and me at the wheel we were oblivious to Willingham and Chatto behind us downing the gallon of cheap wine. Their over-indulgence soon became evident while cruising down the back street of Beach Drive to avoid cops on Hermosa Ave. Hearing the wagon's rear window slide open meant one of the two rear occupants was getting sick; it turned out to be Willingham. Tony awoke with a start and, stimulated by Dave's retching, joined the festivities using the opposite rear slider. And so, the show went into a full color production, the lads from Ocean Beach putting on quite a display for the locals as dual vomiters festooned their streets.

That was it. The night was spent under the Hermosa Pier and, nursing headaches, we headed home the next morning foregoing breakfast. Once again, our boards never entered the Pacific Ocean.

Subsequent escapades up-the-coast suffered similar fates other than one memorable day at Trestles. A glassy summer morning with overhead waves feathering from left to right---we had it to ourselves. It truly was the best day of surfing in my life, one where words are incapable of describing the mix of emotions and exaltation. It was the near equivalent of my wedding day or seeing my son being born in front of me. It was bitchin.

DOWN THE COAST ~ The distance from Ocean Beach to the most dangerous city in the world is less than twenty miles. Once a genteel, polite and welcoming culture, Tijuana is now a combat zone for the cartels averaging multiple homicides daily. In fact, recently cartels took control of the entire city terrorizing inhabitants over a weekend. An act beyond the pale of what we used to find so alluring.

In those times, Mexico's magnetism was irresistible; friendly people, warm water, unspoiled beaches with nice surf breaks, a legal drinking age of 18, where gas tanks could be filled for a couple of dollars. For those so inclined, open night life was abundant with clubs like the Blue Fox, Aloha, and Bambi where a bottle of beer cost a dollar while listening to *sones de México*.

A. Lee Brown

Baja surfing trips typically began with a visit to the Long Bar, an establishment occupying the entire corner of Avenida Revolución and

Ocean Beach Crowd at Tijuana's Long Bar (1964)

4th Street. In the 1950s and early 1960s beach crowds flocked to this special bar where a Windansea surfboard was attached high up on a wall. It was often a place frequented by famous matadors as Carlos Arruza, Manuel Rodriguez ("Manolete') and Jaime Bravo. To avoid the raucousness, the more sedate crowd would congregate a few blocks away at the Hotel Nelson, Convoy Club, or at Caesar's Restaurant where Caesar Cardini created his namesake salad.

On the south side of the international border, or *el otro lado* as Baja Mexico was often called, was this panoramic world of experiences for Americans of all ages. The food was wonderful, music and garments colorful, and while we were careful to stay within prudent limits, there always lurked the necessity for caution.

Before we were married, Kathy and I were frequent visitors to Mexico and while by no means fluent, bring able to somewhat converse helped to open doors with Mexican nationals. Maybe it was for a *corte de pelo* from *el barbero* or perhaps a visit to our favorite *panaderia* for *orejas, bunuelos,* or a large bag of y*oyo pan dulces* or pastries of coconut glued together by raspberry jam. We enjoyed the people, the color, fast moving *Jai Alai,* shopping and even the traffic signs. Not far below Ensenada, for example, was a warning sign on Highway 1 declaring a treacherous curve just around the bend as *una curva muy peligroso,* only to find another sign warning, *Despacio! Curva muy fantastica!*

Speaking of dangerous places, the public swimming beaches of Tijuana were notoriously plagued by rip currents. Sadly, there were no trained, professional *salvavidas* only teenage volunteers bereft of fundamental equipment. These brave kids would patrol, on foot, the dangerous conditions existing from *Plaza de Toros Monumental* for a mile or so to the south, without swim fins or rescue buoys. The most frequent problem typically occurred when a swimmer would ignore a *salvavida's* warning, then need to be rescued at great peril also for the volunteer.

To improve international goodwill and safety, Kathy and I began delivering equipment discarded by the San Diego Lifeguards to these brave volunteers. Loaded with old rescue buoys, landlines, pith helmets, whistles and swim fins we provided what we could to the Salvavidas de Tijuana. Incidentally, the City of Tijuana currently has a well-trained and very professional lifeguard service; a vast improvement over what existed a half-century ago.

Author, age 16, La Mision

Surfing spots in Mexico are identified by their distance in kilometers below the international border along Highway One. In this way, popular surfing beaches became known as K36 or K38. In other instances, destinations were known by geographic proximity to communities like La Misión.

During the 1950s there was no dearth of offbeat humor south of the border. While Windansea and OB surfers had their own favored breaks, we shared a communal love for Punta Banda, La Bufadora and La Mision. As with so much change taking place, these once little known Mexican respites are now chock full of tourists, condos, and tiendas (shops). When these ingredients collide, you can also count on cartels, pistoleros, violence, street drugs, and kidnappings not being far away.

Eventually, the scene got so rancorous that political pressure forced the San Diego Police Department to screen and deny anyone under the age of eighteen to enter Mexico. As a result, young surfers began to seek ways around the embargo. At that time, the international border was a porous, rusted chain-link fence maybe six-foot high extending five miles from the ocean to the official crossing point at San Ysidro.

In 1960, at age nineteen, I drove three passengers and four surfboards down to Imperial Beach; the southernmost tip of the USA. Phil Conger was three years my senior, while Ron Green and Dave Willingham were just as many years younger; it didn't matter, we were all from OB.

Below Imperial Beach we motored along parallel to the border until an opening was spotted in the fence that allowed Ron and Dave, both under 18, access into Mexico. Once inside Mexico, they were to move south to an agreed upon rendezvous spot. The only witnesses to our international transgression were a couple of Mexican nationals whose expressions communicated incredulity that any gringos wanted to sneak into TJ.

Confident the first phase of the plan was underway, Phil and I drove back to the highway then crossed the border into Mexico at San Ysidro. Of course, such a caper today would be absurd, especially in the presence of hi-tech sensory devices and vigilance of the US Border Patrol.

Everything clicked and Phil and I were able to recover our criminal cohorts and camp on the beaches between TJ and Ensenada. Two nights were spent around campfires with other surfers who had used the same opening in the international fence. As was the waterman's way, we dined on fresh delicacies provided by the ocean's bosom. Harmless, fun.

It would be an egregious error to leave the impression that all similar feats were harmless: they were not. As years passed, so did circumstances. More than a few spent a night in jail and three fellow surfers drew their last breath south of the border ---Mark Poitras of Windansea and Mike Kelly and Ron Green from the *Cradle*.

CONTESTS

WESTERN CIVILIZATION HAS VALUED athletic prowess for centuries. Evidence of such admiration dates to the 8th century B.C. when competitive games were held quadrennially on the Peloponnesian peninsula. Tracing the history of surfing, however, isn't so easy. Despite several sources mentioning 12th century Polynesian cave paintings depicting board riding, the first recorded evidence of surfing appears in the ship logs of the HMS Dolphin (1767), and later Captain Cook's voyage to Tahiti aboard the HMS Endeavor (1778). Among scholars, there is little disagreement that wave riding migrated from Polynesia north to the Hawaiian Islands where it was incorporated into their culture.

In 1890, Honolulu welcomed Duke Paoa Kahinu Mokoe Hulikohola Kahanamoku into the world. As a young man, Paoa excelled not only as a surfer but even more so in swimming Having perfected his flutter kick on Waikiki beaches, he was chosen to represent America at the summer Olympics of 1912 in Stockholm winning a Gold Medal in the 100 meters freestyle and a Silver in the 400-meter relay.

About the same time, another Hawaiian, George Freeth, was demonstrating his water skills before onlookers at Venice and Redondo Beaches near Los Angeles. Supported by the railway magnate, Henry Huntington, to help popularize beach sports, Freeth invited the Hawaiian Swim Team to join him. As part of an "Hawaiian Week" promotion in 1916, where both Kahanamoku and Freeth exhibited their surfing water skills at Coronado and Ocean Beach. Within the next decade amateur surfing contests began appearing all along the southern California coastline. In San Diego, a local city lifeguard, Charles Wright, organized---and won---the 1925 North Mission Beach Surfboard Tournament.

Prior to WW II, the Pacific Coast Surf Riding Championship was the dominant board surfing contest. In 1921, the quirky and talented Tom Blake had a chance encounter with Duke Kahanamoku and it changed his life. Moving to the West Coast, Blake became a photographer, author and champion surfer who convinced the Corona

61

del Mar Surfboard Club to sponsor annual championships for the next nine years; first in Newport Beach and later at San Onofre until War II ended the event. Among professionals, Blake is the personality that energized surfing and transitioned it from a quaint Hawaiian sport to a way of life.

As the 1930s progressed, a nascent interest in standup wave riding began to catch on until World War II interrupted everything. At war's end, interest resumed in surfing contests. According to Matt Warshaw's *Encyclopedia of Surfing*, nearly 400 competitive surfing fetes were held between 1954 and 2002.

The purpose here is not to unpack the history of large, sponsored competitions so much as it is to call attention to the impromptu contests that arose daily on the beaches in the 1950s. This was when surfers closely watched each other to judge performance based on two criteria---who had "hair," and who had "style." The results of these evaluations determined an unofficial ranking in the local beach hierarchy.

Having "hair" in a surfer's world is easy to explain. It meant having fortitude to paddle out and take-off in the peak of overhead waves of large, winter storms. Generally speaking, swells of eight feet or higher will substantially thin-out the numbers of surfers considerably. It was one thing to have hair in small surf, but quite another to take off in brutally cold water with no wetsuits or goon cords, and a high risk of injury.

If having hair was the abscissa, then style was the ordinate. During the halcyon days of surfing in the fifties and sixties, these two dimensions were indicators of a surfer's overall ability. Although no formal agreement on form existed, a mastery of basics determined the primary rung. Did the candidate stand erect or crouch for a closer dive to safety? Was the rider able to trim the board for maximum speed while avoiding other obstacles. Could he or she cutback and change directions at any time on the face of a substantial wave.

By and large wave riders of the 1950s were evaluated for their quiver of maneuvers ranging in difficulty. Among these were walking forward to "hang ten" toes on the board's nose. David Kealohalani Nuuhiwa, a respected Hawaiian surfer, was deemed the master of nose riding.

Another crowd pleaser was the ability to switch from left lead to a right foot stance or execute reverse takeoffs, kickouts, 360 spinners, bell ringing and tweaking. A few classic poses became so popular they were associated with the surfer who created them. Capistrano Beach's Mickey Mūnoz was known for his creations of El Telephono, El Spontaneo, El Mysterioso and his most famous, the Quasimoto.

In the summer of 1958, I was on the east coast learning how to tie reverse bowline knots at the U.S. Coast Guard Academy while on the west coast Bruce Brown was sweeping floors for Dale Velzy. Determined to pursue his dream career, Bruce convinced his boss to

sponsor a surf movie and, with $5,000, *Slippery When Wet* made cinematic history. It was filmed in Hawaii and southern California using a cast of five local surfers, one of which was Malibu's Kemp Aaberg.

Despite having never met, Aaberg and I shared similar backgrounds. Born the same year, Kemp in Illinois, and me in Texas, our families relocated about the same time; his to Santa Barbara, mine to Laguna Beach.

As a local surfer of Malibu and Rincon, Aaberg honed his skills to near perfection resulting in appearances in surfing films and magazines. His smooth style of riding was impressive, and represented the sublime of grace, elegance, and respect for the waves. Captured at Pupukea, Hawaii, his classic "soul arch" became the logo for *Surfer Magazine*.

Of course, aside from the daily competitions of surfing, there were other fetes of skill in the *Cradle*. Some events were hilarious, others dangerous; nonetheless the spirit of competition was a huge part of daily affairs in the beach cultures of the mid-twentieth century. In many ways, the nature of these contests provides a rich and colorful insight into the *Cradle's* unique status in American history.

HEAD BUTTING ~ Located between the International border and Ensenada is a favorite watering hole known as the Half Way House. Its popularity is unrivaled and, even today, remains a "must visit" location. As a general rule, patrons are calm, preferring to sip beers and talk about motorcycles, sports, and waves rather than bravado.

There have been notable exceptions, and one of the more hilarious events involved two OB locals: Bob Price and Ron Oldham. They had travelled into Mexico to check on a place owned by Bob's parents.

Finding the cottage intact they climbed the stairs from the beach then entered the Halfway House to sip a few beers and watch the crowd.

Being a weekend, the bar's patronage was already crowded and boisterous. Occupying the table next to Bob and Ron were four muscular men, obviously body builders and, judging from their conversation, probably Angelinos from the San Fernando Valley. Two young women had joined Ron and Bob and soon crude comments wafted across from the biker foursome at the next table. As the language grew coarser and more intentional, Price and Oldham could no longer ignore the incivility. As politely as he could, Bob stood and went to the adjacent table asking them to, in effect, cool it. It didn't work and, in its place, a pack mentality emerged making signs of imminent trouble obvious. Electricity rippled through the room, all heads turned to see what was going to happen next which is when Oldham stood, himself a large and muscled man, and said:

"Hey, fellas, this isn't the way we settle disagreements here?"

"Oh yeah," came an answer, "well tell us big guy what do you have in mind?"

Pointing to his friend, Oldham lowered his voice and replied, "Apparently you guys have never heard about the Halfway House head butting competitions and Bob, here, was last year's champion."

Unsure how to respond, the foursome exchanged glances, and Price's antagonist asked, "Well tell us, how does this work?"

By then, even Price---having no clue where this was going---began to worry. To enhance the tension, the entire bar was sharing an interest in the discussion. "OK," said Ron, "let's go out to the head butting court and settle the matter."

Out they went, the boys from Ocean Beach, four grown men from LA, a crowd of patrons, two bartenders, and a couple of Policia Preventiva, or "Federales." Ron used a stick to draw two lines in the dirt and began to explain the rules.

"Each contestant," he said loudly, "will face his opponent from behind the line and assume a four point stance. When the judge, that's me, counts to three, the contestants will fire across their lines, heads lowered to make contact with his opponent."

Seeing he had everyone's attention, Oldham produced two hats and proclaimed, "Those who think the man from LA will win put a dollar in this hat. And those who think the Champ will retain his title, put a dollar in this other hat." As spectators began to unfold purses and wallets, Ron handed the wager hats to the two Federales who began collecting the bets.

"What do you mean by winning," asked a voice in the crowd.

Oldham smiled. "Usually the fella that coldcocks the other guy wins. If both are loopy, then the first guy to his feet is the winner. In case of disputes, the judge's decision is final."

Going along with Oldham's lead, Price, was apprehensive how this might resolve but it was obviously a matter of hair. After all bets were collected, the judge motioned for silence and began counting in a loud voice, "Uno, Dos, Tres" whereupon the two contestants lurched headlong, their contact producing a sickening crunch. Both men crumpled, their eyes rolling around like ping-pong balls in an air flow. The guy from LA moaned and rolled onto his side in a semi-conscious state while Price's gaze was fixed skyward.

As an "impartial judge," Oldham surveyed each man's status then held up Price's hand declaring him the winner due to the obvious differences in musculature, height, and weight. Protests from the loser's buddies were drowned out by Price's supporters and before the situation could worsen the Federales intervened telling the Angelenos to beat it otherwise *la celda* in Ensenada was in their future.

To this day, Bob Price still holds the Halfway House one and only head butting laurel.

SAND EATING ~ I have no idea what idiot created this one. Even worse, the fact that sand eating could attract willing participants is evidence of the wackiness of those days. It might have had something to do with what was happening on college campuses where swallowing goldfish was a popular way to get a free ticket to fraternity dances? At the foot of Newport Ave., however, the sequel became sand eating. Fortunately, its popularity didn't endure, nor did it catch on at Pacific Beach, La Jolla, or Malibu---further testimony they were smarter than we were.

A field of play was easy to design requiring only beach sand, a judge, and two contestants. Eaters would lay on their sides or perhaps tummies with smooth sand adjacent to a pile of dry beach sand. It was a timed event of ten minutes or until one contestant quit. Once underway, each "gobbler" would take a bite of sand from his pile then deposit it a few inches away onto the smooth surface. There was one disqualifying rule: no vomiting although retching was permissible. The audience would form a *Stadia* around the eaters to cheer and perhaps wager on their favorites while passing tourists stood aghast, speculating among themselves as to what in the hell was taking place.

Yours truly participated only once on the assumption that being a winner might attract wahines. It didn't. Even worse, it took hours to remove the grit embedded in gums behind teeth and under the tongue. Unfortunately, I drew Dave Crower, the undisputed champion of OB sand eaters. At one point, his pile was so much higher than mine, he would periodically stop to smile then just as I was about to achieve parity, he would unlock his jaws like a John Deere drag line to resume moving even larger scoops of sand. There were no prizes for sand eaters but there should have been---a trophy for the stupidest kid on the beach.

BOTTLE CAPS AND PEA SHOOTERS ~ Another relatively dumb, albeit more benign, pastime became popular about 1956. Bottled soft drinks came with metallic, hard-ridged caps, and with practice one could learn to grasp the cap between the thumb and *digitus medius* or third digit. The trick was to hold the cap secure then tilt the forearm back, take aim, and snap the fingers. Many gave up too easily after a few fumbles having the cap fall to their feet. Sharpshooters, however, became able to accurately aim and hit targets as far away as ten yards depending on wind conditions. A variant was to play bottle cap golf using trash cans borrowed from the lifeguards and Speedy Norton.

Despite not attracting spectators, the space between Nancy's juke box and the Cubby Hole became an active war zone with mini flying saucers zinging across the driveway. To be sure, it was another pointless, dumb-ass pastime, yet one providing instant delight to contestants. To this day, a spent bottle cap on the ground is an attractive nuisance to most but impossible to overlook for us who once mastered the game. Nowadays, with not-so-nimble digits, the cartridge is loaded between my arthritic fingers, curious to see if it will still fire.

Even though bottle cap snapping lasted longer that sand eating, it, too, was replaced by pea shooters. Sold in five and dime stores, peashooters were little more than long plastic straws with a slightly larger diameter. Ammo was abundant and  bags of hard, split peas could be loaded into a cheek pouch for rapid discharge like a tommy gun. Sadly, the game morphed to targets. Single shots could make some unwitting person think they'd been stung by some insect but it was more sport to spray victims with volleys.

Jack Calvin convinced me to ride the bus downtown so we could sit in the balcony of the Orpheum Theater and spray the audience below during dark scenes in the movie. It didn't take long for the ushers to figure out trajectories, de-weaponized the shooters, then eject us. Undaunted, Jack modified the sport. He'd hide in the bushes along Catalina Blvd. across from the fire station then wait for a convertible with the top down. It lasted for a while until he hit a fire captain on his way to work who captured Jack and called his parents to retrieve the prisoner. Thankfully, he moved away our sophomore year and took his ingenuity with him.

CLIFF DIVERS ~ There was another popular contest that should have given me pause to think. Diving off the cliffs adjacent to Osprey Point was a favorite attracting not only local wahines, but tourists driving along Sunset Cliffs. For good reason, this activity is now forbidden by law.

Six decades ago, onlookers would gather to watch surfers make use of high tide to exhibit swan dives, cannonballs, and the rare front flip. Abandoned today, but still visible, are three former natural platforms. The lowest, and safest, is about fifteen feet above the swirling water in the open cove below. Ascending five feet higher is another shelf of sandstone and pickleweed. And the ultimate platform is found at the top, at least thirty feet above the water. Two features make this height formidable. Not only are there slightly back sloping cliffs but also submerged rocks requiring divers to make running starts to obtain clearance.

One summer afternoon an audience had assembled to demonstrate our prowess; two of which were known fearless dare devils: Dave Willingham and Donn Shallenberger. From the highest platform, Dave and Donn made their launches with room to spare and a round of applause showed appreciation, then faces turned to me. Moving hastily to foreclose any thought of hairing out, I ran fast and launched a swan dive too far out thus careening off a submerged rock a few feet below the surface. Muted by water, the collision made a nasty scrape instead of a serious injury. Even so, it was a strong reprimand for poor judgement and foreclosed a future diving career.

After a while, cliff diving morphed into bridge jumping. In a way, it became a sort of rite of passage pioneered by Kenny Boyd, Chuck Davis, Chris Town and Donn Shallenberger. Since there were three traffic bridges spanning over Mission Bay this meant alternative venues existed with the one over the ocean channel entrance being the highest. Bridge jumping from these causeways was more hazardous because even with spotters it wasn't easy to tell if a boat was coming under the bridge. Later, as a lifeguard, I'd seen the photos of what happened to those who jumped and came up under the propeller of a power boat: the lacerations were graphic. In fact, one of the best deterrents was to capture these kids and show them the visual and horrific consequences of how others had died.

THE VOMIT MOBILE ~ Sometimes contests moved to the absurd. Such events became even goofier with the arrival of our eligibility to acquire driver's licenses but not maturity. Far and away, one of the most screwy contests was another of Danny's creations.

Although three years my junior, he looked older. A blond, barrel-chested kid, a virtual "mini me" of Bwana Baxley. Quick witted, and a natural athlete, there wasn't much Dan couldn't accomplish if he set his mind to it. Such skill extended to the ocean and, although not a waterman in the traditional sense, he was one of the best board surfers of the day. You couldn't help but like him, other than his tendency to use people; a troublesome part of his nature that probably led him later to become wrapped in a downward spiral of drugs.

The first time Danny came over to my house, I introduced him to my parents, pompadour haircut and all. My mom sized him up as quickly as Kathy's mother had done with me. When he was out of earshot she hissed in my ear, "I don't like that crudball, don't hang around with him." I always wondered why parents felt they had the right to parse their progeny's friends so quickly?

Dan's car at that time was a dented, brown 1940 Dodge sedan. After goofing around one hot, surf-less summer day, he offered a new contest for consideration. Always interested in his inventiveness, the group asked for details.

"It's easy," he said, offering no further specifics.

Someone asked for the rules.

Subduing a smirk, Dan outlined the core of the game noting the day's temperature was nearly 80 degrees. Next came the context. We had to remove our swim trunks, roll up the windows and drive around buck-naked with the Dodge's heater running full blast.

"That's nuts," Brian said, "What's the point, who wins?"

"That's the good news," he answered, "winners are determined by who loses."

"OK," Brian replied, "but how's the loser determined?"

"That's the best part, the first guy to throw up."

Gross as the activity sounded, it was understood by all that here was an opportunity to accumulate significant hair so three younger surfers loaded into the Dodge and off they went. It took less than an hour to determine the loser, although complicating matters was his refusal to exit due to a small crowd of spectators.

THE *SILVER SPRAY* ~ Reconsideration of my mom's judgmental acumen followed another event that Danny instigated in the summer of 1957. It started at the *Cradle*, across the street from Nancy's Burgers where Richard Arnold was weaving a Papale palm frond into a hat. Dan had just come out of the surf and spotted us while drying off. He crossed Abbot Street and sat on the curb with us as Richard continued weaving. It was a feigned interest and before long Dan re-directed the conversation to his innovative contest.

"You guys ever been up on top of the Silver Spray?"
Richard paused, glanced at me then said, "Not that I can remember, why in the hell would anyone want to go up there?"

Smiling, Danny replied, "There's a back way up to the roof and we could sneak up just to look around. The manager's an old guy and the worst he could do is run us off. We each chip in a buck and the last guy to get caught wins the five-dollar pool."

With the metrics almost escaping me I asked, "Hold on, there's only the three of us how can it be a five-buck pot?"

Knowing he had us interested, the Pied Piper of OB lied, "I've already talked with Clamp and McLean and they're in if we are."

Richard and I again exchanged looks until he raised his eyebrow, "Ok, so Brown and I are in but only if Billy and Bob are too."

To which the quick-witted instigator replied, "Hmmm, sounds like a country western song. I'll talk with them and let's meet in the morning at the bottom of the Silver Spray stairs."

In 1919, developer William Dougherty chose this exact spot where OB's original squatter/resident, Capt. Abraham Thomas, had built a shack thirty-five years earlier. Historical significance didn't matter as Dougherty's three-story complex at the end of Narragansett Ave., went up anyway to become the Silver Spray Plunge and Apartments. Contractors made a serious blunder when they decided to pour cement for the foundation. Instead of trucking in commercial sand, to save money they opted for beach sand which---filled with sea salt--- eventually ate away the wooden timbers and rusted steel reinforcements.

At its heyday, the complex had a ballroom, pool tables, and an outside saltwater plunge for divers and swimmers. Over time, the 5,400 square foot swimming pool fell into disuse and was filled with sand making it a perfect miniature gridiron for us to play knee football.

At eleven the next morning, five co-conspirators walked south along the board walk and climbed the back staircase between the aging apartments and the Holiday Courts. As Dan promised, the elderly manager was already snoozing at the front desk allowing easy access to the roof.

Knowing Dan was the un-disputed king of guile, no one questioned his pre-adventure "intel." On the contrary, we fell into line as if captured by a tractor beam from the Starship Enterprise. Moving quietly through the halls, our leader opened an otherwise unremarkable door which, as promised, led to the roof. Stepping into the sunlight like commandos we were treated to unparalleled views of the ocean from Pacific Beach Point to the north and the tip of Point Loma to the south. We also noted, however, there were no guard rails preventing a forty-foot drop to the ground below.

Our exploration of the roof's perimeter changed suddenly. Out of the only doorway emerged the manager's son, "No Neck." He did not resemble his frail father in any regard and, adding to our disquiet he was even more muscular than local myth described. Worse yet, his odd expression made it obvious he was now a participant in "our" game and was already busy redesigning the rules. Confirming our dread, No Neck pulled a padlock from his pocket and in one swift motion locked the door behind him thus eliminating escape other than jumping off the roof.

For a fleeting instant, Dan tried to talk our way out of the dilemma explaining we were merely "lost tourists." Without bothering to listen, No Neck shushed our silver-tongued instigator by grabbing him around the waist like a rodeo rider and telling his prisoner to "can it."

Listening to that exchange produced one of those rare moments of youth when one begins to reassess parental advice. Perhaps I'd given my mother's judgment short shrift.

Our plight worsened when it was obvious that No Neck was studying each of like a predator would its prey. All speculation ended when No Neck demonstrated his speed, strength and agility by snatching McLean as a lizard does a bug. His carnivoral instincts had somehow informed the manager's son that McLean was the weakest link, the slowest of the foursome. No sooner had he grabbed Bob than he turned to Arnold while holding his first victims so firmly they were gasping for air. Bob and Dan appeared to be animals in a trapper's snare where each gesture tightens the wire. With the grace of a ballerina, *il Mostro di OB* added Dick to his mobile prison and turned to me and Bill.

Frankly, we gave up. Having seen the others out maneuvered, we waited to see which way our future would turn. At this point Danny began to plead for his life while I considered volunteering to help.

What happened next convinced me a Merciful Being must rein the universe. Bluto released his captives and made us form an inspection line like petitioners in a medieval court. He told us how disappointed he was with boys our age taking advantage of a kind old man. While he continued, I quit listening. Moments like this are often an epiphany, a point where one can intuit how things might resolve. And thus, the possibility of survival washed away all worries I had about zits, delinquent homework, and girl trouble.

No Neck pulled out a pencil and piece of paper and said, "Ok wise guys, I want your names and addresses." Without blinking, and always honest when confronted by overwhelming authority, I was prepared to supply the requested information. Thankfully, Bill was first in line and Dan's equal of spontaneous imagination. Without so much as a waver in his voice, Clamp told No Neck his name was Bob Baxley and he lived at 3769 Dixon Place, paused then added he was sorry and "would never do it again." Of course, had we been able to see each other's faces, a simultaneous eruption of hysterics would have followed. While the first part of Bill's answer was pure fabrication, the second part was clearly true---rest assured, none of us would ever do this again. In quick order, we each became someone else. Satisfied with our answers, although I suspect No Neck knew exactly what was going on, he un-locked the door and escorted us down the stairs, past his aging, and grinning, father into the passageway leading to freedom and a future. Upon release, we made it to the old saltwater pool now filled with sand. Celebrating our youth, we broke into uncontrollable paroxysms of laughter and rolled in the sand as it absorbed our tears of joy. I can't recall who managed to regain control first, but we ran from that castle of horror as young warriors saved by providence, straight into the Pacific Ocean to cleanse our souls with brine.

Today only two survivors of that contest remain---me and Richard. When we do re-connect on occasion, that day inevitably resurfaces even if we don't mention it. I can never drive down Abbot and turn onto Newport Avenue without sneaking a glance at the Silver Spray.

SHORTS

A NOTHER noun often heard around the beach was the word "Short." It was a pseudonym for automobile, likely originating in some high school auto shop. In those days, hot rodders purchased rebuilt engines that would arrive without essential parts which became known as a "short" block." From that beginning, this word became slang for a car.

Empty wallets comported nicely with the beach's contrarian ethic. As a result, old cars, worn out clothes, and vintage bikes were not only affordable, they transitioned easily into fashion statements. The more damaged and uglier the object, the more bitchin it was.

THE CLAM~ On December 6, 1956, I turned sixteen and drove the family Ford sedan down to the DMV licensing building on Cedar Street. Surprisingly, mom allowed me to solo to the testing center; confident I would be licensed for the return home. Thankfully, the DMV inspector didn't inquire as to how I got there, passed me, and the open road was mine.

Despite the Ford being an aging relic, access to it was not easy. Early on, my mother had discovered it was yet another tool allowing her to leverage desired behavior from her son. On the other hand, Mammo was more liberal with the keys to her 1947 Plymouth, especially since her Texas sons had recently bought her a new Ford sedan. It was what economists like to say, "a positive externality." I inherited my grandmother's Plymouth and, in return, the family had to no longer indulge my incessant whining.

Within twenty-four hours, Gordon Tribby used his oxy-acetylene torch on the front springs to drop the car's front known as the California "rake." The alteration proved to be a mistake. Every bump in the road called for a swerving maneuver to avoid spraying sparks on any driver foolish enough to be behind me. Within weeks the front bumper had to be removed adding to my mother's distrust of her son's judgement. Next, the rear seat was discarded to allow surfboards to be shoved through the trunk while the deck lid was secured with a rope. That is until the time I hit a bump so hard the tie-down snapped thus allowing the trunk lid to rise then close like a Pacific bivalve cutting my surfboard practically in half, thus the short's nickname---the "Clam."

Prone to overheating, I was reluctant to drive the Clam up the coast and, without insurance, Mexico was too scary. Adding to its charm, was the night Bob Bradley threw up in the back seat. Efforts to remedy his transgression with a Pine Sol air freshener only augmented the fragrance thus alerting potential passengers they were better off walking. All in all, my social life began to suffer as word spread about the car's peculiar aroma.

To mom's dismay, the world renown Scripps Institute of Oceanography hired her son as "engineering trainee" right out of high school. At first, I was ecstatic until it became apparent my job was to be a gopher for the lab's short-sleeved, white shirted, pocket protected, technicians. Making matters worse, I had misunderstood the salary terms. What I thought was the princely sum of $2.40 an hour was $240 a month. For 160 hours of running errands and re-stocking resistors, that penciled out to be the same wage I made boxing groceries at Slaveway.

By the end of summer, enough money had been saved to look for Clam's replacement. A pal named Chuck Scott, nicknamed Hummer---a budding artist with a flair for the unusual---bought the Plymouth for $45. The day after he took possession, he slathered its roof with resin then cemented a lawn of dirt clods on the car's roof and spray painted them red. The visual effect made Clam appear to be growing a head of red Irish hair. About the only beneficial result of his artistic creativity was my mother couldn't recognize her own mother's former car being driven around OB.

Not long after, Hummer removed the license plates and abandoned the Clam somewhere on display in La Mesa. In its place, he found a 48 Pontiac that wasn't in bad condition except for its dislocated rear suspension. This oddity, enhanced by a fractured frame member, resulted in the front tires tracking in the driver's lane while the rear end would wander from side to side. He named this marvel of automotive engineering the "U-2" after Gary Powers who's spy plane had just been shot down near the Russian city of Yekaterinburg. Whenever the U-2 would turn onto another street at an intersection, its rear end would swing toward oncoming traffic terrifying drivers.

As an aside, whenever I look at my left hand, I am reminded of Chuck Scott's art. For the princely sum of $35, he melted dental gold and fashioned my wedding ring; a classic blend of innovative design and modern jewelry that Kathy and I have cherished for decades.

THE WOODY ~ Bundling money from the Clam's sale with saved  paychecks, eventually totaled enough to look for a replacement. After a couple of dead-ends, an ad appeared for a woody wagon. It turned out the seller was a surfer I knew from Windansea named Jimmy Stewart who was going away to college and needed dough. For $135, he sold me his 1950 Ford Station wagon. Despite the Woody's sun-faded black paint, balding tires, and exterior wood crying for care, it didn't matter. A surfer's dream of a perfect ride was mine.

History will record that buying that car was simultaneously one of most wonderful and dumbest moments of my youth. Without hesitation, it would haul us down the coast and up to the ski areas at Big Bear; her faithful flathead Ford V-8 never hesitating to respond.

Then it happened. In the summer of 1960, I noticed a clean looking, Ford o'head valve, V-8 engine sitting in Lee Peterson's garage a block or so from our home on Adair Street. He said it was from a wrecked '56 T-bird and offered to sell it for $125; almost what the Woody had cost. A deal was made and knowing little about cars in general---even less about engines---I went to work dismantling the Woody's existing powerplant. Removing the flathead wasn't difficult as two guys from Scripps, who did know what they were doing, bought the motor and yanked it out of the Woody in an afternoon. That's when the trouble began.

Seven months were spent trying to squeeze the replacement motor into the empty, and smaller, engine compartment. Pieces of the frame had to be removed by torch, the oil filter plated over, and sections of the front wheel wells cut to allow access to spark plugs. And, the worst problem was never resolved---how to install carburetor linkage. In the end, a compromise solution was to run a cable wire from the driver's seat, through the firewall, and attach it to the carburetor that had been purchased in haste.

Clueless as to what I was doing, patient friends offered advice. I read everything I could, even talked with some guys in car clubs. Once the reversed polarity issue was understood, ignition soon followed. Yet the biggest problem remained, how to get gasoline vapor into the cylinders without a gas pedal. Eventually, I reconciled with fate and permanently accepted the makeshift wire throttle. By steering with my left hand, the right hand had to do double duty: shift gears and pull the strap wrapped around my right wrist for acceleration. It was a formidable task for an octopus, and in my case required a team to operate the vehicle.

I would steer and, on signal, depress the clutch while Tony Chatto would shift gears and operate the gasoline cable. Any attempt to cruise at a constant speed was impossible. After hours of hazardous practice, and hundreds of petrified pedestrians, we were ready for traffic: or so the team thought.

Able to run the engine for longer periods of time created an overheating problem. The original motor's radiator was adequate but the larger o'head power plant had an unquenchable thirst. At first, this trouble was partially solved by driving only at night but finally a new and bigger radiator had to be installed. Even then, engine heat remained a problem. Ignorant of the fact that oil circulation not only lubricates moving parts but also helps cool the engine, I had removed the oil filter and plated over its mount. While the new radiator helped somewhat, minor overheating still demanded careful attention to weather, distances, and other operating conditions.

Despite setbacks, the pit crew remained loyal and a collective decision was made to try our hand at the local amateur dragstrip known as Hourglass Field (today Marine Corps Air Station, Miramar). Ron Green was in charge of the floor mounted gearshift; Tony Chatto manned the carb linkage from the back seat while I steered and Willingham brought the beer.

We never made it. In fact, we were nowhere close to the raceway when the engine sucked a valve and bled to death spreading its oil all over the highway. It had taken seven months of salary and body blows to convince me it was time to toss in the towel. Words cannot describe the mixed emotions of simultaneous deflation and yet emancipation from a self-created debacle. Standing there looking at the Woody, Ron tried to comfort me saying, "Lee, just think of all the automotive knowledge you've gained." He was right, of course, but I had gained a wisdom far beyond automotive mechanics. Don't engage in projects when you are a witless idiot.

We hitch-hiked back to the *Cradle* sans the Woody. A quick call sold it for $25 to the same guys who had bought the flathead motor. I never made it public that Carroll Shelby was my second cousin since it was obvious I hadn't inherited any of his Texas shade tree mechanic skills.

Ocean Beach was home to a wide variety of infamous shorts. Dave Crower's '32 Chevy terrorized the girl scout campgrounds of the wooded area of Sunset Cliffs. Tom Johnston painted the words, "*Broad Jumper*" on the side of his Olds Rocket 88. Ron Green's 41 Chevy was set on fire in the Osprey parking by bored "pals." And Chatto's '56 VW came home on a flatbed trailer after we slid into oncoming traffic on an icy road going skiing.

BLACK DART ~ Following the Woody fiasco, a sensible 1951 Ford was purchased from my friend Snuffy Herron who was leaving to trek around Europe. Far and away, one of the more lighthearted escapades took place in that sedan known as "Black Dart." It began one summer evening at a beach party at the foot of Hill Street. Tommy Johnston, aka the Bird Man, well over 6' 4" even in Junior High, had met a young wahine with whom he was quite smitten. Her name was Shirley and she opined to Tom that she was stranded and needed a ride to her home in San Clemente. Bird Man asked if I could oblige and, adhering to the beach code of friendship, said, "sure." Since she lived on a north county flower farm, Shirley offered to fill the Ford's tank from her dad's private fuel pump.

Another surfer, John Freitas, joined us so we strapped our boards on the roof and headed toward the Pacific Coast Highway. In the hubbub of things, I overlooked telling my passengers about a missing sparkplug until its psssst, psssst, hissing became impossible to ignore.

Aware of my reputation as an inept mechanic, Freitas asked calmly, "What the hell is that?"

To dampen concern I explained, "Aw, it's ok, a loose sparkplug blew out and stripped the threads so now it's running on five cylinders instead of six."

To access the Pacific Coast Highway from Ocean Beach is a distance of five miles, requiring crossing over two Mission Bay bridges. Given a mile head start from OB to the first causeway bridge the Dart achieved an assault speed of 45 mph. Although the Ford slowed considerably, it successfully summited the first bridge, and we proceeded to the second causeway. Not only was it higher it was also closer, thus disallowing the Dart to achieve the necessary summit speed.

We didn't make it on the first try. Fortunately, at 2 a.m. there were neither witnesses nor cops around so we turned around, returned to  the first bridge for another attempt. Mashing on the accelerator, the Dart again tried to summit. Despite a top speed of 25 mph, the Dart stalled and with a final backfire died ten yards shy of victory. It was clear we were stuck between the two causeways and nothing short of an engine overhaul or tow truck was going to change the situation.

Desperation called for creative strategy. Passengers were deployed slightly below the brink where prior attempts had failed. Alone in the cockpit, I returned to the first bridge, but this time did not turn around and kept the Dart's rear end facing the support crew waiting near the summit. Using the lower gear ratio of reverse, gunned the engine and tried to back straight up the bridge. The Dart made it beyond its highest point and on the verge of stalling the three-person rescue team sprang into action and pushed her over the top. Brimming with *gravitas,* we headed to the flower fields of north county.

But that night the gods still weren't sated. Arriving before dawn, Shirley was eager to enter her house before her parents woke up. Which is why, when the locked gas pump was encountered, she simply smiled, shrugged her shoulders, warned us about the guard dogs and left us at the locked pump.

Running on vapor and sixty cents between us, we got as far as San Clemente hoping to borrow a few bucks from some surfers we knew at Dale Velzy's shop. By mid-morning the famed proprietor was a no show, so with grim resignation we began knocking on doors in the residential area around Avenida Del Mar. The best that three unskilled teen laborers could offer was child labor, or lawn mowing. To our delight, faith in America's landed gentry was partially restored as we were given breakfast, work, and a couple of donations. Tired, but not so weary as to drive past Trestles, we paused to duke a few waves on the way home to OB.

It is an understatement to say that cars were a huge part of American adolescence during the 1950s and early 1960s. What wasn't obvious was the divergence between the role automotive transportation played in places like Omaha or Salt Lake City compared with the coastal communities of San Diego. For that matter, the role of cars in Ocean Beach or La Jolla wasn't at all like the hit songs of the Beach Boys. The life expectancy of our shorts was more accurately measured in hours than years. Many were purchased for less than $50 and easily abandoned for whimsical reasons.

THE BURBAN ~ Beyond doubt, the most bitchin short I ever had was a 1947 De Soto Suburban. A three-seater with leather interior, it

was an eye-catcher that had been an experiment with "fluid drive" transmission allowing it to shift gears either manually or automatically. Of course, in either mode, the weak-kneed, six-cylinder engine made it no dragster. Manning Calhoun sold it to me in 1961 then later begged to buy it back. I agreed---it was part of the code.

OTHER SHORTS ~ Part of the charm of owning inexpensive cars during the 1950s was their dispensability. Drying up the market for old beaters was the existence of a popular event known as "Destruction Derby." Held inland at El Cajon, drivers would crash and bash into each other's beat up jalopies until only the winner was left running.

It was a constant source of delight that migrated to the beach, especially to Windansea where they had their own brand of street side demolition derby. Locale didn't matter whether at public stoplights or beach parking areas. They would ram into each other amidst hilarity. For a while, it seemed the lads from Windansea and the *Cradle* were in competition to see who could perform ever more outlandish modes of destruction. If Tiny Brain Thomas drove Bill Graham's old Chevy into the surf at Windansea, Danny would send his current beater over Sunset Cliffs. If Dick Arnold painted his 39 Ford with Zolatone using a roller, Mel Nevitt would use a flit gun to decorate his aging

A. Lee Brown

Studebaker Champion.

It is commonly thought human craziness correlates with full moons. In the *Cradle,* automotive events could be expected at any time---especially on warm, waveless, summer days. Consider, for example, the wooden forearm and hand with protruding middle finger of Steve Aldridge's panel truck. Since there was no roof, the finger could be displayed at will by his passenger to oncoming traffic. It was great fun until the gesture was extended to an oncoming San Diego Police car by Brian Davis---whose father was a sergeant with SDPD! Before the cops could turn around, Steve turned down a back alley eluding the police on his way to meet his band playing at the Red Garter. Later, the same two officers recognized Steve's truck and waited for him to emerge. Luckily they chuckled with the beach humor while confiscating the wooden digit.

One of the more notorious events took place on an August day in 1958. It was another lackadaisical day with no surf. To break the doldrums, Dave Crower suggested we go "plinking" up in the Miramar canyons not far from Hourglass Field. The biggest hurdle was that although it sounded like fun, none of us had transportation. Crower---Danny's equal in inventiveness---talked a younger kid named Mike into loaning his old Pontiac to "run some errands." Mike was a Hodad who liked to hang around the *Cradle* and didn't hesitate to comply. Armed with .22 single shot rifles, four of us piled in and took off for the Clairmont Plateau a few miles north of San Diego where ample dirt roads provided entry to a large, undeveloped region.

Random shooting soon exhausted viable targets of tin cans and bottles. Determined to save face and support his escapade, Crower startled everyone by shooting the passenger door of Mike's car. He then turned to me, Green, and Chatto wiggling his eyebrows and the contest was on. The "kerplunk" of a round hitting metal was as alluring as tymbal noise is to summer cicadas in search of a mate. Prudence abandoned, a fusillade  peppered Mike's car so when the firing ceased, the old Pontiac resembled the south wall of the Alamo. Even worse, attempting to drive it on flat tires back to the Highway, one came off its rim and with the car lilting to the starboard we realized the folly of the effort. With few alternatives, the rifles were stuffed into pant legs providing an image of four youths sharing the same genetic infirmity. After what seemed like an eternity, our foursome made it back to the *Cradle* where Crower passed a hat for donations then broke the news to Mike offering seven dollars along with an apology.

During those years there were other, equally hilarious, incidents associated with cars. No small aspect of this peculiar pastime was a function of the beach's basic psychology of nonconformity, and the general California attitude that our cars were extensions of personality.

For whatever reasons, the use of cars to create our own *Concours d'elegance* began to wane in the mid-1960s as the Viet Nam war grew in intensity.

A. Lee Brown

CRIBS

A S WE AGED (not to be confused with maturing), the desire to experience new avenues surged. The lucky ones benefitted from parental endowments and went away to college, others joined the military, a few sought jobs or went to community colleges or both. In general, economics dictated that to leave the nest and seek independence required roommates; compatible or not.

And so it was that an initial step was to join with others, to procure an affordable domicile; preferably within the *Cradle*. Known as "Cribs," these accommodations tended to disassemble almost as hastily as they had been created. The net result of Crib hopping provided a ready supply of roommates in constant flux. Cribs held in highest esteem were usually closer to the ocean and, therefore, more expensive. Ones that survived the longest tended to house a small number of roomies willing to share routine chores. On the other hand, most attempts at shared living failed as roomies would eat each other's food, chinch on their share of the rent, or leave dirty dishes for others.

World War II altered the generally accepted beach lifestyles of the 1930s and 1940s to the popular postwar arrangements of the 1950s. One example of the latter was the "Beach Hut" occupied by Don Mellon and Bob Baxley. They were permanent lifeguards posted at Ocean Beach and both had been raised primarily by their mothers. Their waterman skills had been acquired from first generation mentors and as a result their bivouac was the envy of the beach; a habitat well-known for luaus, seafood, music and festive evenings and daytime card games. Living on the beach and off the ocean's bounty seemed to be an ideal way to enjoy what a southern California coastal community had to offer.

Other lifeguards like Mike Considine and Doug Smith occupied similar housing on the north side of the guard station where it, too, offered seemingly non-stop pinocle and two-man beach volleyball.

In my own case, after leaving high school in the late 1950s, several ill-fated efforts to fly the coop were attempted. A first solo was with three fellows I had known since junior high in an apartment on lower

A. Lee Brown

West Point Loma Blvd. This pairing was doomed from the beginning since our school and work shifts never matched nor did we seem to ever have enough money to pay the rent. Following that failed excursion, I recycled home for a while then found a different set of roommates at San Diego State. As the school year ended so did our compact and it was home again.

Things got better in 1961. Another lifeguard, George McGuffie, and I secured a two-room spot above a garage in south Mission Beach. It was ideal, close to work, good neighbors and well-located for fishing and diving off the entrance to Mission Bay's north jetty. George was the perfect roomie, clean, considerate, solvent, and an excellent diver that kept our larder chock full of fresh scallops and lobsters while I did the same with abalone. He didn't drink often, but when he did, I learned why his friends called him "Crazy George." When George was drunk, he was un-predictable, trending toward berserk. Making matters worse, George fell in love with an older woman who was crazier than he was and known around the beach as the "abalone woman." Fortunately, the government resolved my dilemma peacefully as the U.S. Coast Guard called him to active duty. Reconciled to my fate, I moved back to my parents but this time had to sleep in the garage.

THE HOLIDAY HOUSE ~ Easily the most well-known and popular

crib in Ocean Beach was Holiday House. Above the ocean at the foot of Orchard, it was the home of two of OB's more well-known residents: Bruce (Wool King) Westphal and Steve (Nipple Nose) Aldridge later known as the "Mayor of OB." Their crib was a hub of OB's social life during the *Cradle's* halcyon period. Bruce and Steve were handsome devils, quick witted, good athletes and surfers. In addition, they were talented musicians brought together by Steve into a band originally named the Jokers. Aldridge did vocals and keyboard, Bruce strummed the guitar, Charlie Hartranft, blew the sax with a lifeguard mentor of mine, Gregg Widders, on drums. As their

84

popularity spread, so did more upscale gigs which is why the band's name was changed to the "Holidays," hence the crib's title of Holiday House.

These photos capture familiar faces around the *Cradle* in the spring of 1963 at Holiday House. The grinning gentleman appearing is Terry (Boweenie) Bowman who died in 2009 and took a lot of sand with him. Although three years my senior, we instantly became good pals and remained that way for half-a century regardless of long interludes of geographic separation. Terry always had a kind word for all, and was one of the *Cradle's* best ambassadors of the *Kapu* spirit. Aloha, Mahalo, Boweenie.

In the middle photo in the plaid shirt is Steve Herron, nicknamed "Snuffy" after a cartoon character of the time (for which he never

forgave Ramona Bausch). We both remember the day of our first contact as pre-teens on a basketball court at Dana Jr. High in 1953. We were twelve at the time and have shared many experiences over the last 70 years. Steve was also the president of the QWIIGS and my sponsor into the club. Next to Snuffy is Tina Demangos, and on the other side of her is Tom

Fanning, previously discussed, next to Bertie Stevenson.

Appearing in the third photo is Jerry Hembury wearing lifeguard blues. This fellow and I also met in 7th grade, and later were QWIIGS,

and lifeguards. It was no accident one of the restaurants he opened across from the Ocean Beach Lifeguard station was named Qwiigs Bar and Grill.

What's funny is that after a while all of the cribs began to look alike. Even though the domiciles were stationary, their inhabitants were transitory, cycling frequently from one crib to another.

A. Lee Brown

SHALLENBERGER'S ~ Donn Shallenberger had another memorable place in the 4700 block of Del Mar; the home of many spontaneous and wonderful barbeques. The fare was often taken that

 day from nearby coves and prepared within hours. Donn confided that while the Del Mar Street home was leased in his name, he couldn't refuse shelter which is why Kenny Boyd, Tom Chapman, Bob Bier, among others, who shambled in and out.

At one time there were at least half-a-dozen similar homes all within about a quarter mile of each other.

PATCH'S STADIUM ~ At one point, Bob Mulrooney and I lived in a two-bedroom place on Del Mar Street owned by Ron Green's parents. Every Friday, the TGIF regulars would arrive bringing Red Mountain wine to sip while watching the "game." This "contest" involved playing broom ball with Patch, our guineapig. It was serious stuff, played in timed quarters with points being earned by guiding her into opposing trash cans without touching her. It began as an offshoot but when wagering started we got worried. At first, she seemed to enjoy the activity, squealing and running around the living room in anticipation. After a while Bob and I got worried we had created something out of control as more guineapigs came to play. As I recall, Sparky Bishop had an entire herd running underneath his home on Froude Street and he began training a few for the sport.

That was it. When people we didn't know began to arrive bearing their own guinea pigs it was time to dissolve the Friday afternoon contests.

86

LIFEGUARDS
Observe Ne Liberandum (OBSERVE, PREVENT, RESCUE)

MOST AMERICANS THINK of lifeguarding as a high school summer job. Generally speaking, lifesavers tend to be viewed as young men and women who are good swimmers, have American Red Cross first aid certifications, and whose equipment is limited to a Little Bo Peep hook.

In southern California, nothing could be further from the truth. For over a century, professional lifeguarding has been a daunting and often dangerous career involving water safety, law enforcement, and substantial grasp of emergency medicine.

San Diego's professional, full-time, year-round agency was created following a tragedy occurring toward the end of World War I. On May 5, 1918, a large group of off-duty servicemen ignored local warnings and entered turbulent surf at the northern end of Ocean Beach. It was a mistake of horrific proportions as more than sixty well-meaning rescuers tried to help the drowning soldiers. Thirteen people perished, thereby sparking a public clamor for the City's local beaches to be protected by trained lifesavers. In response, the City Council directed its police department to establish a lifeguard division with authority to bring both safety and law enforcement to popular swimming beaches from Point Loma, on the south, to La Jolla on the north.

For the next three decades, San Diego's beaches were watched over by policemen trained for ocean lifesaving missions. Slow at first, beginning with three guards at Ocean Beach, the new service grew in skill and size to its current staff of around 100 fulltime guards who are deputized peace officers and certified Emergency Medical Technicians. During the summer, when crowds often exceed more than 100,000 beach goers, the service is bolstered by another 200 seasonal personnel. Today, more than 1,000 lifeguards work during the summer on California's coastal waters, 300 of whom are on duty during the winter.

A. Lee Brown

In 1947, the San Diego service was transferred to the Parks and Recreation Division and, in 1998, merged with the newly integrated San Diego Fire & Rescue Department---each component having its own chief of operations.

At present, San Diego's lifeguards are responsible for 18 miles of coastline, on duty in seven permanent stations. In addition, the seven mile square Mission Bay Aquatic Park is covered by lifeguard boats and its eight seasonal swimming areas are protected plus two guards working through the night at Lifeguard Control in Quivira Basin.

One of the most respected and long serving water safety operations in the world, the service is also responsible for medical and boating emergencies up to three miles out to sea. More recently, these marine safety officers are encountering both human and contraband smuggling. As a result, specialty teams were created to address river, scuba, and cliff rescues using equipment such as Rescue 44---a 22 ton, multi-purpose truck.

In any given year, San Diego lifeguards will log thousands of ocean rescues, some 50 cliff accidents, investigate 300 boating-related incidents and respond to 4,000 medical needs.

Ok, so that sums up the job of today's lifeguards, but what was it like in the 1950s and why were those men such influential factors in the lives of myself and my peers?

During that time period, the permanent staff was less than a third of what it is today. Rescue "cans" were made out of hard metal, and the "cliff rig" was an undependable 1953 Dodge pickup truck with welded modifications. The modern Lifeguard Control building had yet to be built, and lifeguard headquarters was housed in a building in Belmont Park on Mission Beach erected in 1925.

What was unique about guards in those days, however, was that most all of them were seasoned watermen very familiar with San Diego's coastlines. In fact, over half of the group of elders who were my mentors during the *Cradle's* heyday were professional ocean lifeguards.

A PERSONAL SCARE ~ On January 19, 1964, I was the supervising guard at La Jolla Shores. For days, the entire southern California coast had been pounded by a blustery and forceful winter storm with westerly winds gusting to 30 knots producing large foamy waves making it impossible to see beyond the shore break. Another lifeguard, Tony Ciani, and I were in the patrol jeep when a radio call arrived.

"Shores tower to Unit 2209"

Picking up the mike Tony answered, "2209."

"Proceed Code 2 to White House Rip, possible swimmers in distress south of Scripps Pier."

"Ten-Four," I answered then requested for the stand-by guard, Earl Kreplin, to join us as we passed the tower.

It wasn't unusual for bodysurfers from Scripps Institute of Oceanography to use their lunch break for bodysurfing, even in dangerous conditions. While these men and women were strong ocean swimmers, anyone can get in trouble in 56° water; especially during storm surf.

We picked up the third guard and arrived at the scene where it was obvious we couldn't see anything beyond the frothy, windswept mist. In the meantime, two swimmers were coming out of the water but not the third. Radioing back to the elevated tower and its powerful binoculars, proved to be no help; the tower guard had lost sight of the third person as had his two companions. With no visual contact and time of the essence, Ciani, Kreplin, and I entered the water at fifty-yard intervals.

Wading out with swim fins held high overhead, Earl and I spotted the third body surfer returning to shore between us. Ciani, however, was too far south and not aware the rescue was aborted. Already showing signs of hypothermia, I told Kreplin to take the final swimmer back to Shores tower first aid room while I would go back out to try and locate Ciani.

A. Lee Brown

An ocean lifeguard's worst winter fear is frigid water and large frothy waves that churn the air and limit visibility. It wasn't long before it was impossible to either get further out to sea or return to shore. After having lost a fin, it became a struggle for life with early signs of hypothermia and exhaustion setting in.

At that moment, something lifeguard Bob Baxley had once taught years ago came to mind. Instead of struggling against a strong rip current learn to ride with it. To reinforce this lesson he made us memorize waterman's jingle, *"Use the Rip for a Safe Trip."* In this situation it meant don't waste energy trying to return to the shore or struggle to get outside but swim north toward the Scripps Pier and use the always present rip next to the pier to take me beyond the breaking surfline. It took little effort to reach this marine conveyor belt, then relax while it moved me westward beyond the end of the pier.

La Jolla Shores, 1963, Ciani 4th from left; author far right

Once beyond the breaker line another decision had to be made, either swim for La Jolla Cove, miles distant, or swim south, parallel to the beach. With no rescue craft or helicopter in sight, I headed south. To suppress anxiety, I focused entirely on rhythm, first passing the White House landmark, next the Shores guard station tower and down to the Beach and Tennis Club. The cement runway of the boat launching area interrupted the wave pattern just enough that with a final effort my feet touched bottom. An hour had passed in turbulent frigid water. Over my shoulder, I could see Tony coming in behind me having adopted the identical strategy. On our hands and knees, we threw up together, smiling between retches and glad to be alive.

Only later did a Scripps Pier employee tell me that at one point I was within ten yards of Ciani but conditions were so turbulent we couldn't see each other.

Virtually every permanent ocean lifeguard I know will have at least one similar life threatening experience. Amazingly, however, to my knowledge, only two professional California lifeguards have drowned in the line of duty: Mike Knight, San Diego City Lifeguards (1991) and Ben Carlson, Newport Beach Lifeguards (2014).

A. Lee Brown

KAMU A'O ~ MENTORS

A T THE CORE of the *Cradle's* story, is mentoring. Like so many western traditions, this practice began in ancient Greece 3000 years ago when the King of Ithaca, Odysseus, hired a man named Mentor to guide the development of his son while dad went off to war. In this manner, mentoring was conducted by a wiser, experienced, non-family member willing to share his or her wisdom with a younger protégé.

Down through the ages, this task has changed considerably to the point it is now franchised commercially. In the modern world, mentors have become hired tutors, for specific purposes and whose general task is to groom young professionals, primarily for career advancement.

HISTORIC ROOTS ~ Mentioned previously, my mentors were beach boys, lifeguards, and watermen of the "second generation." These were fellows who had, in turn, been guided by their own prior generation of beach boys and lifeguards. A deep gratitude is owed to these fellows; men who sought to protect and pass along necessary skills to help us navigate the treacherous shoals of adolescence. What they shared went beyond how to surf, dive, and understand basic physical oceanography. Above all else, we were given lessons on setting personal limits, facing adversity, and living by an unwritten code of right and wrong.

HAWAIIAN KAPU ~ Much of what we learned was a modified version of what had been part of Polynesian life for centuries known as "Kings *Kapu*." In its original format, the *Kapu* was a list of what was forbidden to commoners. It also legitimated a three-layered society consisting of: (1) *Ali'i*, or inherited royal elites; (2) *Kahunas,* or priests; and (3) *Makaainana*, or commoners. These rules protected the luxuriance of the *Ali'i* while reducing social rancor. This was nothing new since Europe had also adopted the Divine Right of King's in the 12th century.

The *Kapu* had a huge impact on Hawaiian water sports. For example, only the *Ali'i* could use surfboards longer than 12 feet and made from sturdy Williwilli wood while the *Makaainana*'s boards were shaped from inferior Koa trees. Similar exclusions forbid commoners

93

from wearing certain clothing, eating foods, and enjoying limited entertainment. Penalties for violating the *Kapu* were severe, such as death for any poor devil that accidentally looked into the face of the King, or surfed at his beach.

When King Kamehameha I inherited the throne, he sought to unite all of the Hawaiian Islands and relaxed some aspects of the *Kapu*. After he died in 1819, his favorite wife, Queen Ka'ahumanu, went even further establishing a gentler way of life not based on caste. Keeping her young son (the new King) content with other distractions, she revised many Polynesian traditions. It was about this time, that the role of *Kumu a'o* emerged as one who takes an active part in the education of young Hawaiians by stressing the skills and ethics of a waterman's tradition. Islander mentors were careful to not only impart oceanic skills, but also stress *Lōkahi,* or the unity between the sea and civilization.

Looking back, the importation of the waterman tradition to the mainland's west coast was mostly attributable to southern California beach boys who---as GIs---were stationed in Hawaii during World War II. Those servicemen who surfed and interacted with native Hawaiians were very influenced by the *aloha* spirit. After hostilities ended, they returned to places like Ocean Beach and planted the beach life in fertile sand. The first generation of returning servicemen helped spawn a second generation of *Kumu a'o* and it was these fellows who helped guide my generation, through the 1950s and into the early 1960s.

Of course, this linkage was not universal or organized. As energetic adolescents hanging around the beach, we never had a specific individual as a personal mentor. Instead, we were guided by a dozen or so watermen who adhered to a loosely held mutual pact of unwritten rules passed on by their own guides in the late 1940s. By and large, we learned our watermanship from the second generation of beachboys who exposed us to this wonderful way of life.

Beginning at Pescadero Beach, my cohorts and I were gradually assimilated into the world of beach boys and lifeguards. At first, the lessons focused on water safety, beach etiquette and some fundamental oceanography. These spontaneous tutorials did not occur at preset times or in an organized manner. It wasn't uncommon to learn simply by listening to the banter of older beach boys while standing around a campfire or sitting astride surfboards waiting for the next set of waves.

Simply stated, these individuals were powerful influences to whom we gave deference. Sometimes, Bud Caldwell would show us how to prepare delicious sculpin by being careful to remove its excruciatingly painful thorn spikes. Or the time Hal Krupens improved my abalone diving by demonstrating how to swim upside down under reef ledges where they were attached.

In other instances lessons were often triggered by an event. For example, in 1959, a diver named Bob Pamperin disappeared off La

Doug Smith

Jolla Cove. The consensus was he had been the victim of a great white shark. Leery and concerned about the implications of the incident, we asked Doug Smith about it. In our world, men like Smith commanded respect, seven years my senior he was a permanent lifeguard, beach boy who had grown up in the *Cradle* and served in the U.S. Army. To calm our obvious apprehension, Doug explained that while Whites are the most dangerous sharks in California waters, chances of being attacked are very rare. Taking the lesson further, he said the attack signal to watch for is when a shark lowers its pectoral fins and swims toward you in a zig-zag pattern.

Similar lessons often followed events on the beach. Senior guard Bob Baxley was fond of turning a genuine rescue into a teaching moment. Always concerned for ocean safety, he was relentless in making sure we understood the mechanics of rip currents on sandy beaches and why they were different from rock beaches. One day, after having pulled a young girl out of a robust rip, he gathered several of us together and asked, "Why are rip currents more treacherous at high tide?" After indulging a few incorrect youthful guesses, the waterman explained high tides have larger amounts of water in need of an escape route seaward. "As a result," he continued, "seawater will follow gravity until it finds a depression in the bottom sand then turn seaward." Bwana also made sure we understood there was no such thing as an "undertow," but a situation that happens when an unwary swimmer steps into a depression. No longer able to touch bottom sand, he explained, the victim panics as he is being swept seaward.

Certainly, there were other imperatives as part of our tutelage; most made sense, others could require more rigorous thought. Many of the rules had to do with surfing etiquette and were designed to thwart rude behavior such as language around girls, respect for elders, and always following through on tasks undertaken.

The right-of-way rule while surfing was nuanced and learned primarily via experience. For example, once in my early days of learning the code I was riding a medium size wave at the cliffs toward shore. Two older surfers were paddling out and instead of stopping my ride or trying to ride beyond them, I cut between them. Coming too close, one of the men, I later learned, was Marsh Malcolm, who scolded, "Hey, asseyes, that's number one." I didn't want to find out what was number two!

Another right-of-way violation was dropping into a wave when another surfer was already coming your way. Not only was it rude, but potentially dangerous causing an unanticipated defensive maneuver. In fact, violation of this rule is still a frequent cause of water altercations.

In similar fashion, we were told to always help others in distress. It's one thing to lose your board in small waves, in huge surf it can be life threatening. Bob Simmons was an experienced surfer who drowned in September of 1954 at Windansea. Mark Foo and Sion Milosky were big waves riders from Hawaii who drowned at Mavericks near Half-Moon Bay in 1994 and 2011 respectively. Oahu's north shore wears the undisputed crown of lethality where Ehukai State Park's---known as Banzai Pipeline---has drowned seven surfers.

A classic example of surfers having a selfless obligation to help others took place in the fall of 1961. Dave DeVore, was a senior at Point Loma High and being a strong and excellent surfer, had entered the U.S. Surfing Association's West Coast Championship at Huntington Beach, California. It was a big event and one which, incidentally, had been won the previous year by another friend and neighbor, Dave Willingham (1960's Junior Men's Champion).

A group of surfers was warming up for their heats when DeVore caught a head-high wave, banked left and reached down to perform a rail grab when another surfer entered the same wave and collided with him causing a serious head laceration. Windansea surfer Butch Van Artsdalen witnessed the wreck and pulled the semi-conscious DeVore onto his board and took him to the beach. Despite being a favorite to win that year's competition, he borrowed a car and drove the injured DeVore to the hospital. By the time Dave was stitched and they returned to the contest, Van Artsdalen had been disqualified for missing his heat.

Watching out for each other became a personal lesson in the spring of 1956. I had just turned 16 when a huge swell arrived from the north Pacific. Determined to demonstrate our "hair," Ron Oldham, and I ditched class to give the big surf a go.

Parked above the Garbage reef break at Sunset Cliffs, we watched as sets with faces of 8 to 10 feet rolled in on a regular basis. Although terrified, yet reluctant to admit it, we waxed our boards and paddled out at the foot of Ladera Street. At that age, I could best be described as a scrawny kid, wearing cutoff cotton sweatpants, endowed with rubber band arms and two legs that could vibrate like banjo strings when I was cold. Exchanging faux smiles, Ron and I paddled into an angry sea. Once outside the surf line, we parted ways, being a goofy foot he went south to AB as I stroked toward North Garbage. Cold and scared, I kept my small and light Velzy further asea to ensure safety. Only when I was well beyond the breaking surf line, did it become chillingly apparent---I was alone.

It's striking how oblivious adolescents can be about their welfare until it's too late. Ron was nowhere in sight and the surf was starting to close out in both directions. Suddenly a set of massive waves appeared behind me. Paddling hard for their shoulders the Velzy barely made it over each double overhead face. If I had tried to take off and lost the board it would have been a life-threating, dumb-ass mistake.

Glancing south, Oldham was still nowhere in sight and all I could see were enormous waves in both directions. Overwhelmed with fear, my best bet was to stay asea and try to paddle north to see if there was a safer place to attempt returning to shore. Maybe Pescadero, and if that didn't work, the next place was Ocean Beach with its vigilant and permanent lifeguard station. With glum resignation, the Velzy and I headed north when an odd thought intervened---I wondered what was happening in third period American history.

Dale Velzy had designed my board to make short abrupt turns, not glide over long distances. As a result, it was an exacting struggle just to get even with Luscomb's Point. It was also clear neither Luscomb's break nor No Surf beach were going to be accessible as waves were breaking even further out over the Indicator reef. Eventually, Osprey Point came into view along with a miraculous lull in sets---a window of opportunity! Desperation overruled judgement as I frantically paddled toward shore hoping a rideable wave might appear. About halfway in, a medium wave was building behind me. The swell lifted the Velzy until it began to follow gravity down the face. Under those conditions, it would have been much safer to remain prone on the board, no fancy stuff, no walking the nose, no arching turns, just get the hell into calmer water. But I didn't. Instead, I was beginning to stand just as the board's skeg caught a kelp bundle sending me into the water. The Velzy continued on, eventually reaching shore in a rocky small cove just north of Osprey Point. It was a high stakes gamble with two options---forget the Velzy and swim to the point, or try and recover it then paddle back out to the point. In either case it was an imminently unfair situation being posed to a frightened adolescent. Not only had it taken months of scrimping and saving while bagging groceries at Safeway to purchase the Velzy, it was my identity and most prized possession.

I started swimming toward the cove neglecting to think about an exit strategy. That oversight became a serious problem. Getting to the board was relatively easy, getting back out was not. No matter how hard I tried to break through the nonstop waves, it was useless. Hypothermia was taking over and my situation weakened.

The direness of my ordeal hadn't gone un-noticed as a sizeable crowd was gathering atop the cliffs above. Two men on the edge of

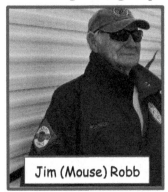

Jim (Mouse) Robb

the crowd remained silent, watching the situation with folded arms. Nodding to one another, they began down an access path leading to Osprey Point. Reaching the water, my rescuers disrobed and swam to me in their BVDs. As they got closer, I recognized Jim (Mouse) Robb and Mike Considine, both former City Lifeguards, well-known beach boys, and excellent watermen. Their calm manner was reassuring as Mike took the Velzy and began paddling out while Mouse led me to the base of the cliffs where high tide waves were crashing. Shouting over the noise, he demonstrated how to deal with approaching waves by turning to face the cliff with legs apart and arms extended to brace against the sandstone cliff. Once a wave had broken over our backs, we'd scamper along the rocky bottom until another wave made it necessary to repeat the drill.

It took a while until all three were safe and the precious Velzy was by my side. I cannot say for sure those men saved my life that day, but their courage instilled a strategic life lesson; one welded into memory and used often years later as a rock guard in La Jolla.

Lt. Mike Considine

As time has moved on, so have Considine and Oldham. When Mouse Robb recently became seriously ill, I made a special trip to see him. Sitting in Jim's living room I tried to share how much his tutelage had helped define my own life. It went without saying we both knew what was coming and he died two weeks later.

Robb and Considine, were of a generation of watermen who had, in turn, learned from their own prior mentors; men I have referred to as "Generation I." Out of this esteemed group, it was my privilege to know personally only two men: Alexander "Bud" Caldwell, and Raymond Leon (Skeeter) Malcolm.

When I was a kid, Caldwell was the Lion of the *Cradle*, a recognized waterman, sailor, and inventive surf board designer. He and his wife

Bud Caldwell

Mary Jane had graduated from San Diego High in 1942 and married soon after. Toward the end of World War II, Bud was a Navy pilot flying a variety of aircraft and later yard manager for Kettenburg Boat works on Shelter Island. His love of the ocean was deep and sincere, allowing him to adapt his skills as a master boat keeper to design and build experimental surfboards.

Despite a sixteen-year difference in ages, our lives crossed frequently. Bud's gentleness was the hallmark of his persona along with an impish grin and willingness to help anyone in need. During the sixty years we knew each other I never heard him utter a swear word or backstab anyone with a snide remark. Bud Caldwell was a gentleman of the first order and a great example of the southern California adaptation of the Hawaiian waterman's code. Among Caldwell's many credits was helping to establish the original Sunset Cliffs Surf Club. One of my most profound *Cradle* memories occurred in 1957, when Bud signed my membership card and handed me a key to the locked gate to one of the best surfing spots on the west coast.

Years later, Kathy and I bought a home across the street from the Caldwell family. It brought great joy to our lives including sailing with him and Mary Jane on their 32-foot Kettenburg sloop, *Onion Truck* plus meeting their kids Janie and Alex.

Two other men were revered around the *Cradle*; the Malcolm brothers. The eldest, Raymond (Skeeter) graduated from PLHS in 1940 and his brother, Marshal (Scooter) followed a decade later. They

were lifeguards who became professional educators and coaches. Both men were also in the elite group of mentors; Skeeter in the first generation, and Marsh in the second.

Skeeter had been a member of the original surfers who frequented Sunset Cliffs in the 1930s and 1940s. His closest friends began calling him "Big Kahuna." When WW II came along, Ensign Malcolm saw action during the horrendous sea battle for Okinawa in 1945 aboard the carrier *Lunga Point*. At war's end, Skeeter returned to

Skeeter Malcolm

lifeguarding while completing his preparation for a career in education. After years of coaching and teaching at Point Loma High, Skeeter Malcolm became a school administrator in charge of several schools around San Diego and never gave up surfing.

Taking his own place in the next generation, Marsh Malcolm was also an outstanding athlete. Whereas Skeeter excelled in basketball, Marsh was an all-star football player whose broken field running earned the nickname "Scooter." Both brothers were ocean lifeguards and Marsh led the Crawford High Colts as varsity head coach for years.

A TURNING POINT ~ For many years Kathy and I maintained a domicile in Point Loma, punctuated by temporary residences elsewhere like Minnesota, England and Texas. As our careers dictated, one could say during that period the Brown family lived "on" the *Cradle* but not "in" it.

The costs of that lifestyle came to a head on a Friday in the spring of 1988. Kathy had gone to Montreal to a medical conference while I met academic obligations in Los Angeles, Houston, and San Francisco.

Returning home exhausted, we poured a glass of wine and began serious parsing.

The lure of careers and income had blinded us to what was really important in life; our kids were growing up fast without us. The answer was easy. We adjusted our lives accordingly and, despite taking whopper pay cuts, it was the best decision we ever made. Soon we were spending more quality time with each other and our kids.

In addition to coaching my son's little league I began surfing again. John Holly shaped me a new board and I was feeling great, riding waves, wearing South Coast T-shirts, and paddling out with former mentors. About the same time, Bud Caldwell began taking me to Tourmaline Canyon where Skeeter, Marsh, and others of all ages would surf early then gather around Skeeter's Travel-All to drink coffee, share donuts, and listen to Hawaiian music. What struck me as especially sweet, was that the group's ages ranged from ten to seventy. A new generation of watermen was in the making.

A. Lee Brown

Four of the second generation OB beach boys (left to right) Rod Luscomb, Rudy Thompson, Bob Mellison, and Don Mellon.

HODADS, JACKET CLUBS, & NIGHT LIFE

H ODADDY ~ NO ONE IS SURE of this word's origin. Like so many "beachy," slang words it was probably Polynesian. Loosely defined, a Hodad was a person, typically male, that hung around a

particular beach, mingling with locals although not addicted to surfing. Even then, if a Hodad occasionally paddled out it wasn't unusual. Along the same lines, Hodads could be passionate watermen, catching fish with hoop nets, diving for abalone, body surfing, and deep-sea fishing.

Both La Jolla and Ocean Beach produced their own unique groups of Hodads---known respectively as Mac Meda Destruction Company and OB Longhorns. Although these assemblages were parallel in time, and anchored in locations barely miles apart, they were very different in patronage and activities.

MAC MEDA DESTRUCTION COMPANY ~ Jack McPherson and Bob Rakeshaw are the acknowledged founders of Mac Meda. The son of a La Jolla surgeon, McPherson worked for the U.S. Postal Service and occasionally surfed at various La Jolla Beaches. His compadre, Rakestraw, was likewise employed in a variety of local jobs.

Where the group's name originated is lost in La Jolla's fog. In fact, locals will usually snigger then say McPherson made up the Mac Meda business to fend off writers and reporters. A few contend it was to honor drinking, destruction, and sex; not necessarily in that order. McPherson's home on La Jolla's Girard Street provided the un-official headquarters although Dave Osborn's Red Mountain Inn, on La Jolla Boulevard, was recognized as its primary drinking/party location. Probably McPherson's most frequent retort to curious queries was that Mac Meda was a Costa Rican fisherman he met years ago.

Mac Meda patrons gathered for raucous parties and heavy drinking coupled with a rejection of bourgeois middle class values. Several times during the year, the organization would produce a "convention," to be held at the end of Sea Lane. As the rowdy crowds increased, so did police surveillance sending leadership in search of greater seclusion. From then on fetes were moved inland either to Carmel Valley's Brown's Ranch land or to some abandoned adobe farm building. Empowered by amplified music, Steppenwolf, the Beach Boys, or Rolling Stones could be heard while revelers fortified themselves with unlimited beer for one dollar; there was never a paucity of strangers for Mac Meda's bacchanals.

Additionally, Mac Medans occasionally engaged in other practices including home destruction and driving Hudson's and old Pontiacs over the cliffs of Torrey Pines.

It helps to understand that what Thomas Wolfe described in *Pumphouse Gang* tended to confuse readers into thinking Mac Meda was comprised of Windansea surfers. Surely there were exceptions, yet the pumphouse gang were mostly Hodads frequenting a hangout a hundred yards south of where surfers congregated along the sea wall across from Windansea's parking lot.

The Windansea "shack" was originally erected in 1947/48 by surfers Woody Ekstrom, Don Okey, John Blankenship, and Fred Kenyon on the sandstone outcrop at the foot of Bonair Street. Over the years, it hosted Hawaiian style luaus despite being damaged and restored several times by storms or vandals. In 2017, the Windansea shack was designated as an official historical landmark.

The Windansea locals were simultaneously known for their excellent and strong wave riders plus their own brand of zaniness as mentioned previously.

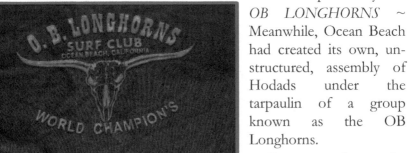

OB LONGHORNS ~ Meanwhile, Ocean Beach had created its own, un-structured, assembly of Hodads under the tarpaulin of a group known as the OB Longhorns.

Rumor attributes the group's name and origin to a conversation in 1960 taking place between four OB locals riding home from class at San Diego Junior College in Chuck Scott's U-2. Talking about his sex life, or lack thereof, Bob Mulrooney commented to his fellow passengers he was really "horny." To which, came a reply, "Yeah Bob, we noticed you do have long horns." Unwilling to let a good pun go by, Snuffy Herron added, "yeah, Bob, you are an O.B. Longhorn!"

Not long after, the odd alliance known as the OB Longhorns melded together to produce unusual parties, contests, and very

competitive teams of track, football, and soft ball. Small at first, its unofficial membership grew substantially but, unlike Mac Meda, the Longhorns remained primarily for friends who had graduated from Point Loma High and known one another for many years. The above photo was taken at one of the group's earliest spontaneous meetings; this one at the San Diego City Refuse site. The sign above declares, *"This Shelter Reserved For Sanitation Crews."* Our transportation that day was Bill Deacon's 1956 Ford Flatbed Truck which, as one can

imagine, engendered many double takes on its way to the dump. Seated on the beer keg is the author while Kathy Brown holds their daughter on the far left. Behind "puppyman" Casey and leaning on the rail is Bob

Sorben, the steady keel in sustaining the OB Longhorns. On the far right (with a head bandana) is Bob, the Crab, Mulrooney. Looking at this piece of OB history is saddening because at least half of the original Longhorns are now grazing in greener pastures. Susie predeceased her husband in 2018 and Bob Sorben went in 2020 also taking a lot of sand with them. Bob's graphic skill was always visible in his annual invitations to Longhorn Christmas Parties. For decades these fiestas were attended robustly by hodads, surfers, badasses, and wahines who had turned into teachers, dentists, pastors, car salesmen, and jailbirds. The lasting bonds of Ocean Beach friendship are perhaps best captured in the longhorn Christmas photos. The following panorama was taken in 2018, Bob Sorben is standing on the far

right while I am on the far left (we both have hands in pockets).

JACKET CLUBS ~ American jacket clubs reached their zenith among teens during the 1950s and shared similarities with the Jets and Sharks of Leonard Bernstein and Stephen Sondheim's *West Side Story.*

Jacket clubs were off-campus organizations bound together by a particular interest of a neighborhood, high school, or hobby. The Oaks, for example, arose from Point Loma's Portuguese community while the Los Chicanos hailed from Old Town's Mexican American roots or the *Gaelics* in the Irish parts of Mission Hills. Nor were these organizations strictly for males since many female social clubs existed such as the RTGs from San Diego High, or the

Coquettes, Demarettes, Ka Anoi, and Debutantes at Point Loma High. Sometimes they were based on cars like Pacific Beach's Amps and Tappets. Others were comprised of school leaders and athletes like the Rogues of Point Loma or the Romans of Hoover High. At the other end were the badass clubs preferring medieval titles like the Barons, Lords, and Nobles.

Out of the *Cradle* emerged the granddaddy jacket club of all. Minutes of the official formative meeting held at Dave Cobb's home are dated March 9, 1939. From this small cluster of socially minded athletes and beach boys came a club that remained active as a PLHS institution for a quarter-century. Its core rested on surfing and the beach had a social dimension as well. Its name was an oddity, tied to its members interest in the opposite sex. In the pre-war times, young

girls were known as "Queens," and boys, who liked girls, were called Queeners. As a result, the secret meaning became: "Q" (queeners), "W" (who), "I" (indulge), "I" (in), "G" (great), "S" (sports). Over the years, more than 160 young men from Point Loma High were initiated into the Qwiigs.

Overall, the jacket clubs of that era were different from the OB Longhorns and La Jolla's Mac Meda Destruction Company. The jacket clubs were typically exclusive in membership, held regular meetings, disciplined by swats administered by a sergeant of arms, and leaders were elected by secret ballot.

NIGHTLIFE ~ By the mid-twentieth century, each San Diego beach community had its own popular pub. In Ocean Beach, the Pacific Shores and Tony's Hat Box were popular although the Bamboo Inn, across from the seawall at the foot of Newport Ave, was the beach crowd's favorite. Seated at the bar, patrons could look west to gaze at sunsets when the bamboo curtains were rolled up. As younger kids we'd sit outside the windows hoping an older guy might pass along a beer for us to split. The Bamboo is no longer in existence nor is Tony's Hat Box (now named Tony's) nor is Pacific Beach's Tugg's Tavern. Although Mission Beach's Pennant and Beachcomber still survive.

At its heyday, the Red Garter had a large following with a dance floor and live music. Found in the heart of OB, on Bacon Street between Lotus and Voltaire, the Garter reigned supreme as a popular night spot. Live music by local bands comprised of PLHS alums like the Jokers with Steve Aldridge (vocals,/keyboard), Bruce Westphal (guitar), Greg Widders (drums), Charlie Hartranft (alto sax), and Steve

A. Lee Brown

Herron (manager). Their music pulsed well into the 1960s.

In 1959, Maynard Heatherly left the San Diego Lifeguard Service, donned a Hawaiian shirt, Panama Hat, lit a cheap cigar and opened a bar across the street from the Crystal Pier in Pacific Beach. Known as *Maynard's By the Sea*, he served ridiculously inexpensive drinks and food. It didn't take long before loyal patrons from all around began to  arrive including not only beach goers but bikers, college kids, and patrons in search of a good time. Long lines formed early on Sunday mornings to pay twenty-five cents for a plate of spaghetti with two slices of buttered bread.

My last time in Maynard's was 1964. Kathy, Tom Fanning, and I had gone to see a karate movie at Ken Cinema in Normal Heights. Afterward, we drove to Maynard's for drinks and dinner. Tom had, delicately said, a tendency to livening things up hence his nickname, "Tommy Cuckoo." Before entering, I beseeched him by explaining my date meant a lot to me and if he felt even a scintilla of craziness coming on to please warn me. A few beers later, he pulled me aside and with wide-eyes whispered, "Lee, I think the worms are coming."

I thanked him, paid the bill, and hustled my future wife out the door. Sure enough, a few minutes later he poured a pitcher of beer on four bikers from the Iron Horsemen. Tommy was one of the smartest fellows I knew, although you needed to be aware of his legendary toggle switch by remembering he'd been arrested almost as many times as he was years old.

Heatherly died unexpectedly in 1966, and the new owner, Jimmy Poulus, sought to extend the tradition but couldn't; the legend folded two years later.

CAPERS & PRANKS

B EACH HUMOR OF THE 1950S isn't easy to characterize. Given its spontaneous and unpredictable nature, one might learn more about quantum physics than look for pattern in the *Cradle's* daily comedy. At best, it might be described as a blend of contrarianism and downright ingenuity.

Doubtlessly, teens across America had their own brand of shenanigans, yet it's unlikely those pranks were a daily staple of life. In a word, the beach wit of those years appeared with such regularity that it would be difficult to duplicate.

DEAD MAN'S BLANKET ~ The permanent lifeguard station at Ocean Beach was where a special rescue vehicle known as the "Cliff Rig" was garaged. Whenever the rig came bursting out of storage with red lights and blaring siren it could only one mean thing---an emergency had occurred, usually south on formidable cliffs.

Cliff runs during summer's tourist season provided a stage for local beach boys. Whenever the cliff rig was called to action a carload of young surfers was sure to follow. Arriving at the scene, the guards would typically grab their equipment and leave the vehicle's warning lights blinking while they made their way down to some unfortunate victim.

One of the more well-rehearsed skits for the beach boy actors was to park across the street, grab a blanket and run over to the abandoned emergency vehicle. That's when Dan would lay down on his back in the street next to the truck as his co-conspirators would use the blanket to cover him from head to toe while leaving left hand exposed.

The prank never failed. As carloads of tourists and looky-loos would slowly drive by gawking at the scene, the corpse's hand would twitch and raise its middle finger in a universal gesture. Over time, the performance developed alternative variations such as slowing sitting up like a draped mummy in an old Bella Lugosi horror film.

Eventually, the lifeguards got wind of what was taking place thus bringing a final curtain call to OB's live street theater.

A. Lee Brown

STINKERS ~ High school graduations are notorious for ingenuity. For example, there's the old marshmallow trick where graduating seniors hide a gooey surprise in their palms to be exchanged with the principal for a diploma. The list is endless and mostly harmless such as playing elevator music over the campus speakers, hiding chickens throughout the campus, or unscrewing lightbulbs all over school the night before.

Point Loma used to hold its graduation ceremony in the Greek Theater on the campus of Madame Tingley's theosophical society. The final graduation in this lovely setting happened to be held for my class of 1959. Several pranksters "borrowed" a small quantity of butyric acid from the school's chemistry lab. It's a fatty "carboxylic" acid produced by anaerobic fermentation found in the colon. On the morning of matriculation, three co-conspirators snuck onto the stage and applied the purloined gooey substance, smelling like puke and poop, to the microphone and its stand. Believe me, no one wanted to shake hands with the team of administrators who took turns encountering the odors of education.

THE PRODUCE SECTION ~ Somewhere around 1957, Richard Arnold coaxed me into a prank that backfired. He thought it was a

 milestone in his determination to hold the crown for different ways to spend idle hours during surf less days.

Despite having heard of this prank before, I'd never been privy to its execution. Apparently, Richard's interest in biology had led him to discover California trapdoor spiders. They are sizeable, timid creatures who remain in their subterrain holes until rains or heavy dews encourage *B. californicum* to emerge along Sunset Cliffs.

Dick's prank involved collecting maybe three or four specimens in a glass jar and taking them to the nearby Food Basket market. Inside the grocery store he would surreptitiously release the arachnids in the produce area then hang around to witness shopper's reactions.

The time I joined him turned out to be disastrous. It didn't take long to capture half-a-dozen of these scary, although non-toxic creatures. The problem arose later upon returning to my car. He'd forgotten to tighten the lid on the jar before placing it on the floor in front of him. Arriving at the Food Basket, we discovered the jar had overturned allowing its inmates to scatter under the seats and into safety.

Despite extensive efforts to locate and extract the little buggers they remained at liberty. Even worse, they began to multiply. One re-emergence, in particular, produced severe penalties. I'd taken a nice girl to the Midway drive-in theater only to have one of Richard's escapees descend from the sun visor, and crawl up her skirt. Word of the incident spread rapidly making my Ford's reputation one of "avoid-at-all-costs" thus sending social life in a downward spiral.

PYROTECHNICS ~ Locale doesn't seem to matter when it comes to making things go "boom." Whether it's overseas or Ocean Beach, some mischievous force seems to compel young boys to experiment with explosives. A corollary to this assertion is that while incendiary devices can be purchased, homemade variants have far more allure. Short fused cherry bombs flushed down toilets were so popular that George Lucas included such a scene in *American Graffiti.* And then there were M-80s lit and launched with Whammo slingshots. The bigger and more powerful the explosive, the greater its allure.

Around the Cradle, dectonics became a veritable testing ground for every imaginable variant; some with hilarious results, some with tragic endings.

THE FRENCH OVEN ~ One of my best friends lived in an apartment above Pescadero Beach. In the summer of 1962, a strikingly beautiful young French woman moved in next door. Despite his best overtures, the mademoiselle remained aloof, turning up her aristocratic Breton nose at the thought of dating a surfer and city fireman. Although they would occasionally pass each other by happenstance, the relationship went nowhere; that is until he put his skills to use.

Knowing where her front door key was hidden, he would slip into her kitchen while she was at work and install a firecracker under the oven's burner in such a way that its fuse would light whenever she tried to bake something. The resulting explosion would send the hapless damsel next door beseeching her fireman neighbor for help. The plan worked for a couple of times, as he would come to her rescue and assure her everything was safe. All went well until the ruse took an unanticipated turn. No longer willing to tolerate the random explosions, she moved to Los Angeles to room with her sister.

THE RED BADGE OF COURAGE ~ In the fall of 1964, four local

111

lads bundled their creative energies to assemble the A-bomb of beach explosives. At the time, Sparkletts was a local water distributor delivering its product to customers in five-gallon glass bottles. Utilizing an empty bottle to serve as an experimental shell casing, the bombardiers replaced H_2O with another liquid: gasoline. A rag soaked with hydrocarbons was then inserted into the bottle's spout. At dusk, the bomb was rolled down to the edge of a natural sinkhole on Sunset Cliffs near Luscomb's reef.

Not knowing what to expect, the support crew withdrew to what they thought would be a safe distance while the pilot ignited the fuse and rolled their creation over the edge. Unexpectedly, the bottle hit the cliff halfway down, shattered, and ignited the volatile vapor. In his own words, the bombardier recalled what happened sixty years ago.

"It was a new moon, very dark. We were unbelievably reckless to have even considered this. I threw the "cocktail," and its carefully fitted towel, with great trepidation. Experientially, it went off with the visual, auditory, and emotional impact of an atom bomb. Instant traumatesque! A "what have we done" moment followed then blind flight back to my 47 woody which I drove away very carefully. We were temporarily blinded by the very high and intense roaring flames so even driving slowly was difficult. We didn't stick around. Back to a beer at our Narragansett crib. I am, as an adult, shocked by the inherent risks...with even the remote possibility that someone could have been down below."

THE WATER BALLOON HOWITZER ~ I've not been able to affirm the creator of this source of summer afternoon entertainment. Apparently, the device required a four-man fire team to accurately control its operation.

The weapon was made of two long strands of pliable surgical tubing  attached to a cloth pocket. The trick was to place a small water balloon in a leather pocket so the gunner could stretch back to aim and launch the missile. Standing next to the battery team, was a fire control director armed with 10/50 binoculars who could correct poorly aimed rounds.

A favorite launch pad was situated on the cliffs adjacent to the Holiday Court cabins with ample downrange beach blankets providing a target rich environment. Rumor had it that toward the end of their campaign, the artillery squad experimented with chunks of ripe watermelon rummaged from the garbage bins behind Swoboda Market.

A. Lee Brown

SEA'S BOUNTY

MOVING FROM LAGUNA BEACH to Ocean Beach in the late 1940s ushered in new challenges. Not only did it mean dealing with new neighbors and school, it also required learning to navigate unfamiliar geography. Fortunately, a neighborhood youngster sensed my angst and volunteered to show me around. Although a year younger, Frank Kamfonik already had a solid grasp of Ocean Beach, loved baseball (later pitched for the Pittsburgh Pirates), and boy howdy, did he know how to fish.

Until then, my angling exposure had been limited to a few times in Laguna Beach fishing with Mammo; my "Auntie Mame" grandmother. Every so often, she'd don that whimsical long-bill fishing cap and we'd drive up to the public docks of Balboa Island where she would demonstrate using live bait to fish with a dropline.

Things were different with Frank. He was serious about fishing for the sole purpose of augmenting his family's pantry. Our first venture was to ride bikes down to where the San Diego Electric Railway once deposited passengers at the foot of Santa Cruz Street. "Right here," he explained, "there used to be a fishing pier and people could step off the trolley to walk out on the pier to fish."

Next, we pedaled north on Cable Street, through the OB village, and to where remnants of the original Bacon Street bridge remained. Built in 1914, the span once connected Ocean Beach with Mission Beach. Frank explained the bridge was being torn down in sections so Mission Bay boaters could have an access to the sea. The northern section had already been removed while the southern section, from the end of Cable Street and into the Mission Bay channel, remained intact. Until this structure was removed, anglers of all ages and sizes sought to catch fish in the flowing channel seawater.

Water wise for his age, Frank said the strong "flood" currents were incoming high tides and then reversed to form "ebb" current flowing back out to the sea. He added that the older and more experienced anglers used rods and reels to fish on the bridge's east side during flood currents. Then when the tide began to recede, they would move to the west side to fish the ebbing current. This shift allowed older kids with homemade spears to quickly occupy the abandoned side of the pier in hopes of snagging halibut, bass, or bonito; more often they landed stingrays, skates, or opaleye.

Underneath the bridge were even younger kids hanging from its cross-members and using green drop lines. Making a dour face, my guide said, "This is where we would be if we wanted to fish from the bridge." With a smile and wink, he pointed to the rocky rip-rap adjacent to the bridge, adding, "That's where we'll fish tomorrow."

The next morning, Frank rigged a pole for me and we returned to the bridge. Casting a line into the channel while balancing on the rip-rap took practice at first but I did catch a small opaleye perch. Although unaware of it at that moment, this was a first baby-step into the waterman's world.

A year or so later, an attempt was made to create my own "Hawaiian Sling." Dixieline Lumber provided a six foot pole of #2 pine and Stanley Andrews Sporting Goods did the same with a metal, three prong spear point. After several days of sanding and varnish, the spearfork was fastened on one end and surgical tubing lashed to the other end. It was summertime, and I was anxious to try it out. Practicing in the back yard everything worked. Moby Dick look out, a new Ahab had arrived.

Not long afterwards, my first attempts at spear fishing involved bus trips to La Jolla Cove. My parents weren't too worried knowing their son was already competent to navigate public transportation. All that was necessary to get to La Jolla was making sure the spear tips were corked and enough coins were in possession to buy transfers. Sometimes Frank would go with me, often not, since he was busy playing Little League.

The green grass above the Cove provided a perfect, shaded, hangout for kids my age, most of them from La Jolla. Although too young to date, I met a nice girl named Suzanne who spoke French and was being sent to school in Switzerland every winter. It was heartbreaking when she left for Zurich but we did manage to write for a while as pen pals. It was also a first taste of social reality because Suzanne later wrote that her father didn't want her hanging around with some kid from Ocean Beach.

There were other reasons for preferring the Cove. Its rocky shore meant crystal clear water for diving and, although it had city lifeguards on duty, there were few dangers as it was a very safe place---most of the time. Since it was against the law to bring spearguns or slings into

the Cove, the best ocean access was from Alligator Head Point on the Cove's west end. At first, I'd watch how experienced divers would put on their fins first, and then dive into an incoming swell while holding the mask and snorkel in one hand and the spear pole upright in the other hand. Never once did it cross my consciousness that a decade later I, too, would be a permanent guard watching over this fabulous setting.

The Cove was mesmerizing. Golden Garibaldi fish were everywhere swimming just above the swirling eel grass. For several subsequent visits I was content to spend the day talking with Suzanne and snorkeling around the Cove's outer limits learning to flutter kick the new fins without diving down. It took a while to gain confidence, but eventually I did muster the courage to dive for the bottom. Taking a deep breath, then using a diver's entry with silent fins, I slid below the surface. About five or six feet down, however, the increased pressure began to hurt my eardrums so the experiment was abandoned.

Perhaps most disturbing was learning the wooden spear I had worked so hard to make didn't go very far in saltwater, plus it tended to have a mind of its own going off in unpredictable ways. In fact, the pole always wanted to return to the surface as quickly as possible. One trauma happened toward the end of that summer while trying to climb back up Alligator Point in stronger than usual currents. Wave action washed me across the rock shredding hands and knees badly.

Over the years, not only did Ron Green and I begin to surf, but our beachboy mentors extended our grasp of how to harvest the sea's bounty by teaching us how to throw hoop nets, pry with ab irons and properly make a Hawaiian sling. One of my prize possessions was a 24.5" inch, single band, Arbelete speargun; an aluminum invention designed by the French Olympic swimmer Rene Cavalero in 1941.

Of course, famous divers like Jack Prodanovich had the skill to design and build their own wooden spearguns, considered nowadays as works of art. Although I frequently saw this master waterman in the halls of Point Loma High, where he worked, I did not know him personally.

The most desired delicacy of Pacific inshore seafood is the California spiny lobster. Thriving in abundance from Point Arguello near Lompoc as far south as Baja California, Mexico, these clawless, decapods have sweeter meat than their east coast cousins. Which is one of the reasons they were overfished mercilessly for commercial purposes, with catches sometimes exceeding 600,000 pounds a season. Today, lobster fishing is strictly regulated beginning in October and closing mid-March. No lobster can be kept with a "carapace" measurement of less than 3 ¼ inches nor can a diver have more than seven in possession.

A similar fate faced abalone, a sub-species of *gastropods* (sea snails) once abundant in Southern California coastal waters from Point Conception to Bahia de Magdalena in Mexico. After near decimation by commercial divers using hooker rigs California Fish & Game in 1996 declared all species of abalone off limits. Despite this bold legal measure, it was apparently too late and the sub-species have continued to decline.

Luau's can be traced back to 1819 when King Kamehameha II organized the celebration to mark the end of the Hawaiian *Kapu* rule forbidding men and women from eating meals together. The word, itself, is translated to mean "fresh taro tops," referring to an important plant in Polynesian and Hawaiian cultures. Looking somewhat like a sweet potato, its root, or "coam," is mashed to make *Poi* while the plant's leaves, or "luau," are blended in a variety of ways to supplement an Islander's diet. As testimony to the sacred place this leafy vegetable has in Hawaiian lore is its mention in the Island's creation chant known as the *Kumulipo:* a folk poem explaining Hawaii's origins, rules, and rituals. Traditionally, a Hawaiian luau would serve a main dish of *Kalua* pig (*Pua'a*) cooked below ground in a rock oven, or Imu, using burning wood, porous lava rock and damp banana leaves to steam and smoke the main dish. Hours later it was served with finger foods of fruits and vegetables.

During *Cradle's* heyday, the end of summer was celebrated with an OB Luau. In keeping with the beach boys determination to live in unison with their coastal marine playground, the event followed a

Polynesian tradition. As young kids, we were not invited to the luaus held next to the OB lifeguard station, although should we help dig the trench, erect palm fronds and other assorted tasks we could hang around.

A previous attempt at an Ocean Beach luau tried to cook a Kalua pig in an Imu didn't go so well. From then on, OB luau's replaced a pig with lobster, crab, fish and abalone dishes harvested from nearby reefs. Music was supplied by locals and their ukuleles. As the summers of the mid-1950s passed, the annual fete was moved to Baxley and Mellon's cottage kitchen.

As it is with most good things, the heart and tradition of the OB luau ebbed and disappeared by 1960. Today, things are very different and if one were to Google the word "luau," the screen is flooded with ads for party favors, gags, garments, and other supplies for a successful backyard party including recipes for fruit kabobs, pineapple upside down cupcakes, Hawaiian hot dogs, and Aloha burgers.

A. Lee Brown

HIGH COUNTRY

IN THE LATE 1940s, *Cradle* regulars began discovering a fresh and alternate activity---high mountains and snow skiing. Although in its American infancy, snow skiing quickly resonated with southern California's surf ethic and by 1950 its allure was irresistible. Despite skiing and surfing being activities performed at vastly different altitudes and conditions, they shared much in common. Both sports required physical strength, dexterity, and a sense of balance. What it takes to turn and trim a surfboard in overhead waves paralleled the skills necessary to guide a pair of skiis safely down steep slopes covered with fresh powder snow.

Adding to the magnetism between coastal and alpine activities, was a mutual sense of natural wonder. Whether it was pure waves breaking over submerged reefs or being amidst craggy mountains, both touched nature and brought a sense of wonder. In addition to geographic similarities, these pastimes shared a socio-economic dimension as well: a suspicion and disregard of bourgeoise values.

As with many elements of the *Cradle,* generations played a big role. Don Mellon, for example, was a second-generation mentor, and one of my guides, yet he speaks with reverence about his own mentors as Robert Penwarden and John Kowal. In his own words, Mellon described how Kowal introduced young beach boys to ski mountaineering.

"Jon Kowal bought skiis, boots and poles for Mouse Robb, Bob Woodall, Sonny Maggoria, Bruce Westphal and me. Marsh already had a pair from his older brother Skeeter. We all promised to pay Jon back with our paper route money. Our first ski trip was to Snow Valley on New Year's Day, 1948. Jon crammed all five of us into his parent's old Packard and none of us, except Kowal had ever been in snow. We struggled with the rope tow falling all over the place. Being yelled at by experts didn't faze us. Towards the end of the day, we could hold a snow plow enough to get down the tiny hill without falling which was a very big deal!"

In my case, I was the classic, day late, dollar short kid which is why it wasn't surprising my peers were already well along in their skiing apprenticeship. Up until then, my vision of going skiing had been

121

limited to Hollywood silver screen stars like David Niven gliding elegantly down Italian slopes accompanied by beautiful women who drove Ferraris.

Nevertheless, it was impossible not to be intrigued by buddies swapping adventures about local ski areas in the San Bernardino and San Gabriel Mountains.

My chance came in 1958, when one of my closest friends, Sparky Bishop, volunteered to take me skiing over the Christmas holiday. We got as far as San Bernardino only to learn the local ski lifts were closed due to lack of snow. Undeterred, Bishop didn't hesitate to push on another 300 miles north into the High Sierra.

We arrived in Mammoth sometime after midnight and nearly froze sleeping in his Ford ranch wagon. Dawn arrived none too soon and brought with it both a new panorama and instant infatuation. I was hooked for life.

Like most things, economics were troublesome. Elite resorts were (and remain so today) famous for expensive accommodations, costly equipment, high priced lift tickets and women wearing svelte attire crafted by Willy Bogner. But skiing was ripe for exploitation by the ingenuity of surfers, most of whom were always on the brink of abject destitution. We found affordable quarters at Ed's Beds where three dollars bought a cot for the night and a shower in the morning. Two La Jolla fellas told us how to sneak into the San Diego Ski Club Quonset hut after dark along with a serious warning to be out before dawn. They also explained lift tickets could be earned by showing up at the base of Broadway Run and ask for a lift crew supervisor named Ted. In exchange for 3 hours of ski-packing and snow shoveling, Ted gave us a lift ticket and breakfast. Such tips were invaluable for neophytes. One of the best was how to plug an extension cord into the Texaco station's outside AC plug to energize a portable small heater so one could sleep in his car.

Our alternative to the tony ski shops was to ransack San Diego's Goodwill and Salvation Army stores for sartorial splendor. As with most things in the *Cradle*, the more non-conforming, hilarious and gauche the more bitchin. Used jackets and parkas were abundant. Although ski pants were scarce, my mother was able to sew ankle zippers onto a pair of woolen army trousers making them into ski pants. Hooded sweatshirts over flannel long sleeved shirts fit the bill while gloves were another matter. In a word, there was a certain pride associated with being able to ski fairly well while sporting cheesy duds in contrast to the fashionable, trendy set.

Transportation presented a more formidable problem because most of us were underage and couldn't drive during the early and mid-nineteen fifties. As a result, this meant beseeching either parents or  mentors for trips to the local mountain ski areas. Dave Willingham's dad was unwavering in his willingness to haul half-a-dozen adolescents one hundred miles to places like Snow Valley or Snow Summit. After a day of thrills and spills, he'd drive us down, past San Bernardino, and head west along Highland Avenue to The Mug. From the outside, the eatery rivaled a county juvenile hall, although inside a good-sized plate of spaghetti served family style could be bought for a dollar. It was a wonderful way to finish off a memorable day.

By the second winter season, enough money had been set aside to buy equipment. Although we were the same ages, Dick Arnold was, as usual, a step ahead of me in his grasp of ski lore. Aware of my growing fascination with mountaineering, Richard took me to a small ski shop recently opened in La Jolla. It was a cozy little place on Girard, not far from the Cove with Swiss doorbells that tinkled a welcome whenever a customer entered the merchant's front door.

Aside from the shop's initial charm, recollections of that day still produce a grimace. My original mistake was disclosing my meager budget to the proprietor. That declaration brought a smile to his face which was, in actuality, more like a smirk. With a nod of his head, he beckoned us to the shop's back room where he said the "real" deals could be found. Stacked against a wall were a number of used skiis and he proceeded to "help" find equipment for my body size and ability.

"Any skiis that you can reach their tips," he said, "would be just perfect." I picked out a couple he rejected as "too short."

In fact, every pair I liked were, for some reason, "not for me" until I finally came to two skiis he probably wanted me to buy from the beginning: a pair of wooden, camber-less 220 cm Kneissels better suited for Wilt Chamberlin than a kook/teen skier from Ocean Beach.

Adding flourish to the ensemble, were two Kastinger, single layer, lace up boots so broken down not only could I ski in them but play tennis as well. And for the *Pièce de résistance*, the merchant produced two, shoulder high checkerboard bamboo poles with enormous baskets. Flashing his disingenuous grin, he said, "they are perfect for you young man."

Looking more like a rodeo clown that a downhill racer, Mike Kelly, Danny Banker, and I ventured to a family ski area above Pasadena named Mt. Waterman. On the first downhill run, a large sitzmark swallowed my Kneissels which augured into the hole's opposite bank. The ancient Cubco cable bindings didn't release as I pitched forward snapping off the tip of one ski; at least it wasn't a tibia. Even more scary, one of the bamboo poles splintered and skewered my parka like a jousting lance---inches away from puncturing my lungs. Unable to ski down to the base, the patrol put me on an empty chair compelling me to display my ineptitude and endure the giggles and smirks of passing uphill skiers.

Undiminished, an attraction to high mountains and skiing continued to grow. After graduating from high school, the job with Scripps Institute of Oceanography provided enough salary to pay for a partial college tuition, a couple of ski trips, and some decent equipment. By 1961, I had made friends with several Windansea guys who were also avid skiers. Typically, five of us would cram ourselves and gear into Larry's 1956 four door Chevrolet and split the gas bill for the drive to Mammoth. Upon the near dawn arrival, we'd go separate ways then reassemble Sunday afternoon for the ride home.

One of those trips still brings a smile. Jim Tejada was a surfer from Windansea and a regular passenger on the weekend Mammoth trips. One Friday it was time to go and when I knocked on his door to help tote gear down to the car is when "it" happened. Opening the door was one of the most strikingly beautiful women I'd ever seen. She smiled and said, "Just a moment, Jimmy will be right here." Before I could stop staring, he appeared, loaded with ski stuff, and we walked back down to the others. Anticipating my question, he offered, "Yes, that's my sister Raquel---she's trying to break into Hollywood using the stage name of Welch."

JUNE MOUNTAIN ~ Following graduation from Point Loma High, Danny moved further along into a skiing career. His success surprised no one from the *Cradle* because he was one of most gifted natural athletes of our group. After a stint in Aspen, Banker became a certified

Far West ski instructor and while working at Alta he met Toby von Eau, who had, himself, trained under Junior Bonous, the acknowledged "pioneer of the American ski industry." With his own reputation gaining respect, von Eau had been hired to head up the ski school of a new resort in the High Sierra named June Mountain. Impressed with Dan's skiing and teaching ability, von Eau asked the kid from OB to be his new Assistant Director of the June Mountain Ski School a few miles north of Mammoth.

In the summer of 1962, Dan called saying he was in town for a couple of days and could I join him for breakfast at Sulek's Waffle shop in Ocean Beach. Not sure what was up, we met the next morning. Following the usual chit-chat, Dan began describing how June Mountain was an up and coming opportunity and wanted to know if I would like to apprentice over holidays as a volunteer ski patrolman as well as bunk up with him during those times. Thrilled with the prospect, the offer was accepted.

When the first winter storm arrived, the trip to June Mountain was harrowing, requiring chains the last 100 miles. The next morning, we toodled around town and then up the mountain. That afternoon, Dan took me to the home of Hart Nathan Cook, his wife Diane, and their three sons. Unknown to me, I was standing before a man who would be a major influence in my life.

After dinner that night, the three of us went into the parlor and discussed the ski patrol. Cappy was impressed with my first responder training and background but it was also apparent that I had a lot to learn about mountaineering. One way to resolve this issue was for me to "shadow" Cook as much as possible and do the same with the two permanent patrolmen already hired.

Cappy was a man of many talents. While at Stanford, he had been a starting linebacker in the 1952 Rose bowl game against Illinois. Finding academic life unfulfilling, Cook assembled a packer outfit in Tuolumne County while competing in rodeos as a saddle bronc rider. Still in his early 20s, Cook enlisted in the US Army, was sent to Korea, then, as a sergeant, to Garmisch, Germany to head up the Army's recreational ski facility at the site of the 1936 winter Olympics. As a ski instructor and head of the patrol, Cook turned to racing on the

European FIS circuit and once took a horrendous fall in the infamous and grueling Kandahar downhill only to walk away from it unharmed. After discharge, Cook returned to the Sierra working at first for the US Park Service and later as director of the ski patrol and race coach for the Dodge Ridge resort where his kids won the Junior Nationals. It wasn't long before the U.S. Forest Service recognized his leadership skills and grasp of mountain life promoting him to Assistant Manager and Snow Ranger for the Mono Lake region. As an aside he was a solid country western vocalist and guitar player.

In constant contact with the owner of Mammoth Mountain, Dave McCoy began to appreciate Cook's skills and temperament. When Bud Hayward got approval to open June Mountain, McCoy urged the new owner to hire Cappy as outside manager and he did.

And this is how I met this mentor of mentors. Cappy was a rock of a man, enormous physical strength, afraid of nothing, unfazed by cold weather, and experienced with how everything works from diesel trucks to ski lifts. At the same time, he had a delightful and subtle sense of humor, possessed an infectious tenderness, and was a model leader.

Working alongside him during those winter holidays helped me become a confident and stronger skier as well as grow into manhood. He taught me how to handle TNT, build snow fences, and evacuate injured skiers. Meeting Cappy was a turning point in my life.

Four years earlier, I had dislocated my right shoulder and it was becoming easier to do it again and again as the subscapularis tendon weakened. Toward the end of that volunteer ski season, I took a bad tumble in deep snow at the top of the "Face" of June Mountain. It was the 9th time my right shoulder had popped out of its glenohumeral joint and only surgery could repair the chronic condition.

At the end of the summer I graduated from college and a surgeon repaired my shoulder. With Kathy's blessing I returned to June Mountain to become its third paid patrolman. Approaching Thanksgiving, Cappy called and said the mountain had enough snow to open and I should to come up. He also mentioned a few complications that had arisen.

"Hmmm, what kind?" I asked.

"Well," he said, "Mike was jailed and Larry was drafted, you will be the senior patroller."

This was scary news to me. Although confident of my medical preparation, having a seasoned command of the other mountain operations was a bit of a stretch.

Cappy continued, "It seems the Forest Service also wants us to increase staff to five patrollers because of the new lift and terrain."

Just bitchin, I thought. *Not only am I a neophyte but will be responsible for leadership.*

Cappy anticipated my concern asking if I knew any lifeguards with advanced first aid certifications that are also OK skiers?

And that's how I became the first official Patrol Leader at June Mountain Ski resort. It's also how June Mtn. became known as "OB North." In quick order, I hired Gary Hottenstein, Ed Redman, John Wishon, and Vern Quillan all from Ocean Beach. Since Gary and I, along with another fellow named Ray Golden, were lifeguards, the three if us roomed together.

For a couple of seasons, we worked from dawn to dusk six days a week earning a couple of bucks an hour along with meals. Eating four meals a day my weight maintained at 175 and living at 8,000 feet insured excellent physical condition.

I learned many things from Cappy about endurance, patience, self-confidence and, most importantly, to finish what you start.

Cappy Cook had been a wonderful mentor. He possessed an uncanny ability to sense when to give advice and when it was better to listen.

One very cold midwinter morning in 1965, we were alone in the ski patrol room dressing for some avalanche work when he asked, "OK, so what's been troubling you?"

An honest question from a genuine friend can never be unanswered, "Cap, I love this job and everything it has given me, my biggest fear is that by holding on to it I'll miss the chance for a very happy life."

He had suspected it was "girl trouble" all along. Cap put his belongings into the ski locker, and turned to me saying, "Lee, you gotta do what's right for you. If you don't, and things go wrong, you'll never forgive yourself." He'd met Kathy and understood she was a huge factor in my life. He also knew instinctually it would be cathartic to voice my internal conflict: the patrol was a job I loved yet staying with it meant a possibility of losing her. He nodded accordingly, and there was no more maudlin chit-chat. We finished bundling up, stepped into a blizzard, and rode Chair 3 to 10,212 feet above sea level to see if we could start an avalanche on the cornice of Sunset Bowl.

Hottenstein and Ed Redman were already there and glad to see us. At first, we tried to tease the beginning of a slide by skiing across the cornice top one patrolman at a time, trying to jump start the loaded cornice while ropes belayed us to security. That didn't work so next we skied below the overhang and placed TNT into the wall at twenty-foot intervals The explosives were wired in parallel to ignite simultaneously so we skied down and rode the chair back up to the top of the cornice where Cook ignited the explosives. No dice, the frozen danger was stubborn.

It was dangerous work. Frustrated and frozen all four of us skied down to the main chalet to warm up. Half-way through breakfast the avalanche let loose on its own, shaking the chalet like a seismic event and thunderous roar. Cappy never paused from his pancakes. For me the incident was a personal epiphany and that night I wrote a letter of resignation.

Returning to the *Cradle,* Kathy and I married a year later. In the meantime Cappy had become the General Manager of the Ski Incline resort on the Nevada side of Lake Tahoe. We skied together once

more, knowing it might be a long time, if ever, before we saw each other again.

Hart Nathan Cook died from complications of Alzheimer's in 2009 and is buried above his beloved Mono Lake. It wasn't until 2018 I found his grave near Lee Vining. It's apparent his *E Clampus Vitus,* pals come up periodically to maintain the site, paint the rocks, and place a new flag in the dirt. It seems that Hart Nathan Cook was held in such high esteem he had achieved the revered status of *Exalted Grand Humbug.*

PART III ~ *DIASPORA*

A. Lee Brown

BEGINNING OF THE END

O N NOVEMBER 12, 1942, Winston Churchill stood before a
gathering of dignitaries at Mansion House in downtown
London. His spoken words were memorable when---in the midst of
the most violent episode in human history---he told his audience, "This
is not the end. It is not even the beginning of the end, but it is, perhaps,
the end of the beginning." Churchill's statement had a profound effect
and almost a century later, on October 1, 1966, I, too, bore witness to
the end of a beginning: the *Cradle* was about to fall.

By the mid-1960s, most of my friends had scattered. Richard Arnold
was an MP in the US Army trying to convince his superior that China
beach needed lifeguards. To help in that endeavor I was sending him
the training manuals for permanent San Diego Lifeguards.

Bill Clamp was in the Air Force somewhere in Spain fixing jets and
playing tennis while Bob McLean was a hard hat diver in the Navy
standing watch in the Far Pacific. Ron Oldham was a green beret
billeted in the jungles of Central America and the Air Force had made
Bob Mulrooney into a Russian interpreter so he could listen to Soviet
pilots from his base in Turkey. Tommy Johnston got married and
stayed in school to finish his MFA at UC Santa Barbara then become
Chair of the Art Department at Western Washington University.

Jerry Hembury and I had stayed on with the City Lifeguards until
he hung up his fins to launch a career in the restaurant trade. Yours
truly, got married and kept chugging away at graduate school by
moving to Minnesota.

The same could be said for younger cohorts who were also either
in the military, like Bob Jenson, Brian Davis, the Chapman brothers,
and Butch Richardson, or had moved to the Islands. A few were in a
war of their own caught in the grasp of mind-bending drugs. A couple
of others survived those challenges to complete college or found jobs
and were getting on with their lives. Their places in the *Cradle's* lore
were rapidly being moved aside by hundreds of new faces sitting
astride boards between Sunset Cliffs and Ocean Beach.

In 1964, the International Surfing Federation held its first
competition in Manly Beach, Australia to determine the best surfers in

131

the world. Held in the northern suburbs of Sydney it was a huge success so a 2nd World Championship was set for Kon Tiki Beach in Lima, Peru.

To our dismay, the ISF chose Ocean Beach, California for the 3rd world surfing contest. It was a big boost for America and set to begin the last week of September with the final competitions taking place on the first weekend in October. The *Cradle* was abuzz when it was also made public the ABC Wide World of Sports would be covering the event and Duke Kahanamoku would be part of the pageantry.

Crowds began gathering early in anticipation of the finals. Those familiar with what was at stake understood it would be a clash between two entirely different styles of wave riding and generations. The traditional graceful California style of elegant maneuvering exemplified by the nose-riding of David Nu'uhiwa, would be pitted against the aggressive, turn and burn Australians. Then, to most everyone's shock Nu'uhiwa was disqualified during the preliminary heats; he had been unable to make the five minimum wave rides necessary to advance.

FRIDAY, 6OCT1966

Early in the morning of the first final round, I reported for work at Lifeguard Control, disappointed about being unable to witness any of the festivities about to begin at Ocean Beach. Climbing the stairs into the ready room, Greg Widders' voice was animated as he answered multiple incoming calls to switchboard. Although Greg graduated from Point Loma High while I was still in 9th grade, he had become a close friend and another one of my guides.

With a few minutes to spare before going out on patrol, I climbed the stairs to the communications control deck to see Greg. We had just started to chat when the Service's radio barked, "Unit 2201 to Lifeguard Control." It was Lt. Bob Shea's well-known voice.

Opening the transmitter, Greg answered, "Go ahead 2201"

"Who's on standby?" Shea asked.

"Brown, me and two more guards to arrive in a few minutes."

Hmmm, I thought, this doesn't sound good, bad things always start like this. Shea was an historic figure, not only with SDLGS but known to practically every professional guard in southern California both for the textbook he had written and his fearlessness in dangerous situations. Lt. Bob Shea's mastery of oceanic skills qualified him as a "waterman" nonpareil. It wasn't only his muscular, 6' 2" physical stature that made him formidable, but his prowess of everything having to do with the sea.

The radio spoke again, "It looks as if the attendance at OB is going to be much larger than we thought and more guards are needed for crowd control. Since you and Brown are familiar with OB, put somebody else on dispatch and both of you meet me on the front steps."

By then, Greg and I were staring at each other with smiling approval. Our first reaction was like Br'er Rabbit's famous response when being caught by Br'er Fox---"Oh lawdy, please don't throw me into that briar patch." Afterall all, getting paid to walk the familiar sands of our youth, ogle pretty girls, and see the best surfers in the world, easily topped long hours in a patrol boat dealing with angry water skiers.

Shea dropped us off at the OB guard tower and it was obvious this wasn't going to be what we had hoped. Everywhere, people were crammed in close proximity, an incubator for drunken mishaps, strangers trampling each other's towels, blanket thefts, medical

emergencies and too much sun.

Even so, at least beach rowdyism was better than it had been a few years earlier. That had been a time when unruly behavior between surfers, tourists and residents was so bad, the City Council verged on limiting surfing to certain areas and hours of the day. Taking matters into their own hands, surfers from the *Cradle* to La Jolla were able to turn the tide by policing themselves and appearing before public officials to assert it wasn't necessary to take drastic steps.

Nevertheless, tens of thousands were already on the beach, with more arriving. Odds were, it was going to be more of a spectacle than light hearted day. Fortunately, my seniority earned a position of observing from the main tower and not in a jeep amidst a restless crowd.

At that instant, I was unaware a watershed moment was about to occur, an insight leading to a major pivot in the direction of my life. Something far more significant than a clash of surfing styles was taking place. The Americans were performing in their traditional, graceful manner that David Nu'uhiwa once described as "blending" with the wave. Before the day was over, it was a style that would earn Jock Sutherland (Hawaii) and Corky Carroll (California), second and third place trophies respectively.

The day, however, belonged to Nat Young who, at age 19, dominated the contest with his self-proclaimed "involvement" technique. On his self-made 9' 4" board named "Magic Sam," Young's powerful turns and snappy maneuvers made other contestants appear predictable, stale, perhaps even "boring." Using a narrowed stance, the tall Australian adopted a crouch that was both exciting and functional. Young's response upon hearing Nu'uhiwa's earlier statement said it all, "…I don't want to blend in with anything."

Watching the Australian rip and dominate the waves was similar to a reaction I once had as a ski patrolman watching younger skiers slash through fresh powder listening to Jimi Hendrix on portable cassettes. Both in skiing and surfing a different world was arriving portending changes in language, etiquette, style and ethics.

Years later, at age 55, I was surfing at this very beach, the temple of my youth, when some young punk speared me in the back with his board while we were riding the same wave. Seeing I was astonished, he taunted, "Go back to where-ever you came from." The incident was so disturbing I didn't bother to answer, "…from six blocks away."

Somehow Nat Young's performance brought everything into focus---nothing was going to be as it was. All those cherished experiences of youth, times nurtured by the sea and mentors were slipping away. The magnitude of that realization is difficult to put into words except to say the bough had broken and the cradle was falling.

Certainly, I am not so naïve that I don't know I am beginning to sound like my father-in-law; things do change, that is only natural.

As the decades passed, the Brown family evolved without tragedy or undue hardship. After Shelby and Tracey finished college and were on their own, mom and dad sought seasons and altitude. After researching and visiting towns in Wyoming, Montana, Utah and

Colorado we returned to the heart of the northern Rockies. Ketchum, Idaho, is a small and unique place while shares a similar code with the *Cradle*. Sun Valley is a world class ski destination created by Averill Harriman 1936. Today it remains the playground of both Hollywood, presidents, and famous writers living shoulder to shoulder with working class folks all of who enjoy its natural beauty and community spirit.

Shelby   Kathy   Lee   Tracey

Kathy swapped her career in medicine to work in a local gourmet kitchen store and volunteer for the Community Library and Hospice. My existence shifted from academe to being an honest in-the-stream hydrologist at first with The Nature Conservancy and, later, as a regional manager for Idaho Water Engineering.

As time went by, the sea's rapture again beckoned so a Beneteau sloop, *Coquette,* was acquired and slipped in Port Townsend, on the Juan de Fuca Strait. From there, it was an easy passage (well not always easy) to the glorious waters of the San Juan and Canadian Gulf Islands,

Eventually, health, and age drew us to our roots. After spending two wonderful decades in the shadows of the Sawtooth Mountains it was time to be back with friends and family. One thing for sure, we had learned to live life with a deep sense of awe, joy, and wonder.

Aloha, Mahalo

A. Lee Brown

ABOUT THE AUTHOR

Born in Texas and raised in Ocean Beach, California, Lee Brown fell in love with the Pacific Ocean at an early age. It was an affair that began in elementary school and grew stronger over time. His original exposure to the sea came in junior high and subsequently became a way of life.

After spending the summer of 1958 at US Coast Guard Academy he returned to graduate from Point Loma High (1959). Instead of returning to Connecticut, Lee accepted a job with Scripps Institute of Oceanography only to learn he was employed in a secret laboratory engaged in defense research. In 1960, Brown prepared for and passed the tests to become an ocean lifeguard with the City of San Diego.

For a decade, he patrolled the bays and beaches of San Diego as a year-round professional lifeguard. It was a platform allowing him to marry Kathy Jones begin a family, and complete two university degrees,

In 1969, America was disassembling over the war in Vietnam and Brown was fortunate to obtain a faculty position with Grossmont College and, soon after, also with San Diego State University.

Over subsequent years, Lee completed a doctorate in hydrology and water resources, became Dean of Science at Grossmont College while his research was published journals, texts, scientific papers and, more recently, fiction. His work has been acknowledged by an Outstanding Educator of America Award (1972), a Fulbright Scholar to England (1972-73), and San Diego State's Outstanding Faculty Award (1996) and supported by organizations like the Ford, and National Science Foundations, Idaho Humanities Council, and the Western Governors Association.

Dr. Kathryn Brown became a clinical geneticist with Scripps Clinic and on the faculty of UCSD. In the late 1980s they moved to the northern Rockies of Idaho where Lee was hired as a hydrologist with The Nature Conservancy and later joined Idaho Water Engineering. After twenty years in the Rockies, they returned to the San Diego area to be closer with family where his most recent novel (*The Varsity*) was published in 2021.

ASSOCIATE COHORTS, POINT LOMA HIGH

Tom Chapman ('62), William Chapman ('65), Sam Cody ('63), Mark Denney ('60), Dave DeVore ('62), Pete Franklin ('62), Jan Gosewisch ('61), Bob Henry ('61, John Holly ('61), Bob Jensen ('62), Steve LaDow ('60), John Maggio ('60), Ken McCrobie ('63), Jerry McHenry ('61), Bob Mussen ('61), Dave Pollock (64), Donn Shallenberger ('61), Chris Town ('61)

Deceased: Danny Banker ('61), Kenny Boyd ('62), Tony Chatto ('61), Dave Crower ('61), Chuck Davis ('61), Fred Delaney ('60), Ron Green ('62), Mike Hatcher ('61), Butch Richardson ('60) Ewart Thompson ('62), Dave Willingham ('62)

A final piece of due respect is called for. Although the fellows mentioned above are referred to as "Associate Cohorts," this reference is a bit misleading. While it is true these men are all younger than I am, most of them were as close---if not closer---than my own cohorts in the Point Loma Class of 1959. On the whole, they were far better surfers than I was (two were certified champions), and a couple of them became professional lifeguards. In a word, we were pals and age differences didn't matter during the *Cradle's* heyday.

CREDITS

Page 4 California Report, "State of Student Mental Wellness" (2022)

Page 19 "The Pottery Shack," Laguna Beach Historical Society

Page 20 "Eiler Larsen," Laguna Beach Greeter, WIKIPEDIA

Page 25 Author on Silver Creek, Idaho

Page 30 Jim Maruodis & Clint Carey (permission from Steve Aldridge)

Page 39 Ocean Beach Lifeguard Tower (1955), City of San Diego Historical Archives

Page 41 "Tres Qwiigs," photo by author

Page 42 "Associate Cohorts," photo by author

Page 44 City of San Diego, " *Sunset Cliffs Natural Park Master Plan, 2005*," Figure 2, Vicinity Map 21

Page 46 Print courtesy of Don Mellon

Page 50 Gabby Pahinui, *"The Gabby Pahinui Band" Volume 1 (cover 1973)*

Page 52 Ocean Beach surfers, (by Steve Aldridge)
        52 Windansea surfers, source unknown

Page 54 Flexible Flyer, Leslie Sands blog, "Hound by the Sea", (2019)

Page 56 Dewey Weber logo, Copyright Dewey Weber

Page 58 Tijuana Long Bar by Jerry Hembury, (1962)

Page 59 La Mision, Baja by Author, (1958)

Page 62 Duke Kahanamoku Special Exhibit, *Juice Magazine #78,* (2015)

Page 63 Mickey Munoz; Matt Warshaw, *Encyclopedia of Surfing,* page 485
        63 Kemp Aaberg's, "Soul Arch," logo for *Surfer Magazine* (1964-2020)

Page 64 Half Way House Restaurant, permission by photographer

A. Lee Brown

Page 67 Huron Plainsman, South Dakota; Mark Smith, "The Green Tomato Robbery," (2020)

Page 75 Beverly Hills Car Club, www.beverlyhillscarclub.com

Page 77 1951 Ford Custom Deluxe, www.fastlanecars.com

Page 78 Ingraham Street Bridge into Crown Point, City of San Diego Historical Archive

Page 79 1947 DeSoto Suburban by Manning Calhoun

Page 80 Ford Coupe driven by Clyde Barrow and Bonnie Parker, WIKIPEDIA

Page 84 Holiday House photo by Steve Aldridge, 1963

Page 85,86 Partygoers at Holiday House photo by Steve Aldridge, (1963)

Page 86 Del Mar Street residence of Donn Shallenberger by author

Page 87 San Diego Lifeguard badge, photo by author

Page 88 Rescue Unit 44, San Diego Lifeguard Service, City of San Diego, www.sandiego.gov/lifeguards/equip

Page 90 La Jolla Shores lifeguards, photo by author, (1963)

Page 95 Doug Smith, photo by author

Page 98 Jim Robb, photo by author

Page 99 Bud Caldwell, photo by Alex Caldwell
      99 Mike Considine, photo by Sharon Considine

Page 100 Ray (Skeeter) Malcolm by Marsh Malcolm

Page 102 Second generation by Don Mellon

Page 103 MacMeda Destruction Company logo www.macmedadestruction.com

Page 104 OB Longhorns logo, photo by author

Page 105 OB Longhorns meeting at San Diego Refuse, photo by author (1969)
105 Invitation to annual Longhorn Reunion by Bob Sorben

Page 106 OB Longhorn Christmas party 2018 by Bob Sorben (far right and author far left, both with hands in their pockets)
106 Los Chicanos Jacket Club logo, www.sandiegofreepress.org by Maria Garcia, (2015)
106 The Rogues of Point Loma High by Jon Cunningham, (1956)

Page 107 Qwiigs Jacket photo by author (1958)

Page 108 Maynard Heatherly, see Mac Meda (above) page 124

Page 110 www.venturapestcontrol.com

Page 112 www.timitreeballoonlauncher.com

Page 117 www.californiabeaches.com/beach/la-jolla-cove-beach/

Page 118 www.fisheries.noaa.gov/species/green-abalone

Page 123 The Mug, *San Bernardino Sun,* (2015)

Page 125 Dan Banker and author (1964)

Page 128 Cappy Cook's headstone, photo by author, (2021)

Page 133 3rd World Championships Crowd of 1966, *OBRAG* by Fred Gormlie, (August 2022)

Page 135 Author and family Sun Valley, Idaho (2003);
135 Sloop Coquette clearing Point Loma, photo by author (2014)

Made in the USA
Monee, IL
08 February 2023

26583910R00085